Diary of the Way

Special Text by

Yukiso
Yamamoto
Lily Siou
Andrew
Lum

Photographs and Commentary by Ira Lerner

Diary of the Way

Three Paths to Enlightenment

A Ridge Press Book

A & W Visual Library, New York

Editor-in-Chief: Jerry Mason
Editor: Adolph Suehsdorf
Art Director: Albert Squillace
Project Art Director: Harry Brocke
Associate Editor: Ronne Peltzman
Associate Editor: Joan Fisher
Art Associate: David Namias
Art Associate: Nancy Louie
Art Production: Doris Mullane

For Mr. Lerner:
Production Manager: Hryszko
Photographic Printing and Film Processing: Marti Corder
Transcriptions: Gayla Gould, Deborah J. Grady, Marilyn Miller
Chinese theater make-up by Elizabeth Wichmann.

Quotations by Lao-tzu on pp. 42, 47, and 55 from
The Way of Life According to Lao-tzu, reprinted with permission of
The John Day Company, publisher. Copyright © 1944 by Witter Bynner,
copyright renewed 1972 by Dorothy Chauvenet and Paul Horgan.
Quotation by Tut-Tut on p. 69 from *The Wisdom of Kung Fu* by Michael Minick,
reprinted with permission of William Morrow & Co., Inc.
Quotation by Lao-tzu on p. 75 from *Tao Te Ching,* by Lao-tzu,
translated by Gia-fu Feng and Jane English.
Copyright © 1972 by Gia-fu Feng and Jane English,
reprinted by permission of Alfred A. Knopf, Inc.

Prepared and produced by The Ridge Press.
Library of Congress Catalog Card Number: 76-49804
ISBN 0-89104-055-2 (hardcover)
ISBN 0-89104-054-5 (paperback)

Printed in the United States of America.

For my Mother, Father, and Teachers

Yukiso
Yamamoto

Lily Siou

Andrew
Lum

Evolution of a Diary

Diary of the Way elucidates the thoughts and philosophies of three modern masters of Oriental arts. All three masters share an insight into "the Way" of life. "The Way," a term originating in Taoist philosophy, has deep and special meaning in the cultures of China and Japan. It has been described as the path to enlightenment, a fine-tuning of the self in harmony with the universe through a mystical, not-to-be-explained system of metaphysics. Lao-tzu himself, the founding father of Taoism, taught that eternal truths cannot be put into words. Because of this belief, the masters of the Way make their points obliquely, through parable and implication, and often through seemingly nonsensical stories. One such story tells of a young monk's search to find the Way.

Encountering a master along a mountain path early one morning, the monk asks, "What is the Way?"

"Oh, what a fine mountain this is," replies the master.

"But I do not ask you about the mountain, I ask about the Way!"

"If you cannot see the mountain," says the master, "you cannot expect to reach the Way."

To some this story may have no intrinsic value. But to the Taoist philosopher its meaning is apparent.

It expresses the Taoist belief that the desire to achieve enlightenment is sufficient to keep one from ever reaching it. The young monk's desire to reach the Way is so blinding that he cannot appreciate the fine mountain before him.

The achievement of enlightenment in Taoism is not at all a rational process. It is nonrational, unexplainable, and intuitive. It has been said that enlightenment can be attained, but cannot be taught. Because the masters of the Way believe this to be true, their teachings do not attempt to show the Way, but to put the student in a state where he can abandon logic and make the great leap upward into enlightenment.

Legend has it that the sage Lao-tzu was immaculately conceived from a shooting star and carried in his mother's womb for sixty-two years. Born white haired, in the sixth century B.C., he grew younger as time passed. Despite the folklore surrounding Lao-tzu, most Chinese historians agree that he did exist and that the writings attributed to him are indeed his. It is said that Lao-tzu, saddened by the ways of men, rode off on a water buffalo into the Great Desert, beyond the boundaries of civilization. Upon reaching the great wall in northwestern China, he was persuaded by the gatekeeper, Yin Hsi, to set down the principles of his philosophy. Lao-tzu did so with great reluctance, because of his conviction that no vocabulary exists to explicate the eternal truths of the Way. Thus, he began with this statement: "The Tao [Way] that can be told of is not the eternal Tao."

This work came to be known as the *Tao Te Ching, The Classic of the Way and Its Virtues.* The *Tao Te Ching,* together with the works of Chuang-tzu, a later disciple, are the two major sources of Taoist philosophy. They have influenced Chinese thought and culture for more than two thousand years. Today translations of these works have extended their influence even further.

Exactly what is a master of the Way? Who is he (or she)? And what does he know about the Way that we don't know? Furthermore, can such a master exist in a modern, Western society? If he can, perhaps this indicates that the master's knowledge is applicable to present-day living. If so, perhaps one may benefit from this knowledge.

The three masters of this *Diary of the Way* are Yukiso Yamamoto, master of *Aikido*; Lily Siou, master of *Chi Kung* and doctor of acupuncture and Chinese herbal medicine; and Andrew Lum, master of *Tai Chi Chuan.* The arts of Aikido, Chi Kung, and Tai Chi Chuan focus on the development of *chi.* Chi, or *ki* in Japanese, is the word used to refer to spiritual energy. Lily Siou calls it the "unseen life force." The concept of chi is closely related to Taoist philosophy. Therefore, the arts which study chi are also immersed in Taoist thought.

The word "master" is subject to much interpretation. In Aikido one is given the title of master after being reviewed by a board of high-ranking instructors, or by receiving the title from one who is already a very high-ranking master. In Tai Chi and Chi Kung titles are not formally granted. But even here certain instructors are referred to as masters. It is safe to say that in all three cases the title of master is conferred by mutual consent, either by the consent of a review board or by an unwritten agreement of one's peers. It is possible, of course, for colleagues to disagree as to whether a certain person is indeed a master. It is also possible to establish oneself as a master by attracting a group of followers who agree that you are their master. The word "master," however, does not represent an absolute value of any kind.

There were many criteria used for choosing the masters in *Diary of the Way*. Orientals refer to certain techniques in the arts as "twenty-year techniques," meaning that one must practice at least that long to master them. Accordingly, only persons with formal training for more than twenty years were considered as subjects for this book. A second criterion was that all three persons must be excellent teachers.

The title given to the masters of the Chinese and Japanese arts is "teacher." To be a fine teacher is part of the essential nature of the true master. Thirdly, each master had to possess a strongly developed chi, the unseen life force.

In my search for such masters I began by observing their students. It didn't matter how skillful a master himself might be, if he did not have good students he had not yet reached the level of mastery for which I was searching. When one enters the teaching hall of a fine master there is a positive feeling which permeates one's being. This sensation is the flow of chi radiated by both students and master. In modern vernacular one might say that the room was filled with "good vibrations."

These good vibrations can be felt by all who enter the master's classroom. The existence of a strong chi in the master's classroom testifies both to his own possession of chi and to his ability to teach its laws to his students.

Yukiso
Yamamoto

was born in Hiroshima on May 18, 1904. He has been teaching martial arts and their philosophy for more than fifty years. His first contact with the arts came at age fourteen, when he studied judo in high school. Judo is an art of self-defense employing the principles of movement, balance, and leverage. Yamamoto's instructor taught him that judo is a gentle art in which knowledge, self-discipline, and being supple enable one to overcome the limits of physical strength. "Gentle, always be gentle. That's what my judo instructor taught us," Yamamoto recalls. This is a lesson that Yamamoto learned well and it has greatly influenced him all his life.

At the age of nineteen, after he had become a judo instructor, he left Japan to join his parents in Hawaii. There he continued his study. His physical aptitude in acquiring the disciplines of judo was so pronounced, and his devotion to his daily tasks so unremitting, that he attained the high judo rank of *Rokodan* while still in his early forties. Rokodan is the sixth of ten possible degrees of black belt which can be attained. Such high ranking confers upon one the title of master. This title

is achieved by very few who study the arts, and even then usually in old age.

At the age of forty-nine, Yamamoto met Tohei Sensei, a most gifted teacher of Aikido, who was visiting Hawaii from Japan. Aikido, as Yamamoto learned, involves breathing and meditation techniques, and a method of self-defense founded in the ideology of nonviolence. Aikido movements constitute a highly effective means of self-defense, but even so the objective of Aikido is to unify mind and body, and promote the flow of spiritual energy.

Tohei, who had heard of Yamamoto's prowess in the art of judo, let it be known that Yamamoto would be welcome to attend his demonstrations of Aikido. Yamamoto, Tohei's senior by sixteen years, was much impressed by the younger man and with Aikido. (He had good reason to be impressed: in time Tohei Sensei became the highest-ranking Aikido master in the world.)

It might be thought that the title of master would incline one to feelings of superiority. Not in Yamamoto. His character is invulnerable to the promptings of false pride and conceit. His desire for new knowledge has never ceased. And so, despite his eminence in judo, and his mature age, he decided after

his encounter with Tohei to pursue the study of Aikido. Tohei Sensei gladly accepted Yamamoto as his new student and, in an almost unprecedented achievement, Yamamoto eventually became the chief instructor of Aikido for the State of Hawaii. For his mastery of the art he was again awarded the extremely high rank of Rokodan.

Lily Siou

was barely six years old when she was taken in by the Master Chang San Fu of the Tai Hsuan Taoist Monastery in Kiangsi Province. She was accepted as a Taoist disciple, studying the ways of nature and their relationship to man, as well as acupuncture, herbal medicine, and the ancient Chinese classic, *I Ching.*

After ten years of training she was sent by Master Chang to the Chinese Medical Hospital College in Soochow, near Shanghai. There she graduated as a traditional Chinese doctor of acupuncture and herbs after four years of schooling and a one-year internship. She then was appointed a resident doctor of the same hospital college. A year later Lily Siou enrolled in Hong Kong Chinese University, where she earned a doctorate for her work on the *I Ching.* Since that time she has pursued her studies of the ancient arts with dedication.

Chi Kung is probably the most ancient art embracing the concept of chi. It is believed that the many arts of chi development which exist today have their roots in Chi Kung. Chi Kung is a system of body control in which even the minutest mechanisms, such as oxygen level, heart rate, body temperature, and antibody level can be consciously controlled.

Acupuncture and herbal medicine, studied as part of Chi Kung, are also based on concepts of developing one's chi. Acupuncturists believe that the flow of chi can be stimulated and regulated by the insertion of needles at key points of the body.

Lily Siou has been known to become so engrossed in her work that she has literally gone for several weeks without eating. Certainly such a routine would be physically extreme for the ordinary person. The principles sustaining her are to be found in a further understanding of Chi Kung and its related arts. To help promote this understanding in the Western world, Lily Siou traveled to Hawaii as a master of Chi Kung. She has since established a following of ardent disciples.

Andrew Lum,

Lum, master of Tai Chi Chuan and the Tao style of martial arts, was born on the Hawaiian island of Oahu, where he has lived most of his life. When Lum was a small boy his health was very poor. A relative suggested that he be taught a martial art to improve his condition. At seven he began to study the Tao style under Master Lum Tai Yung.

When Lum was twelve he had already become such a fine student that Lum Tai Yung made him an assistant instructor. At twenty-two, after receiving his Bachelor of Arts degree from the University of Hawaii, Lum expanded his studies to include the Yang style of Tai Chi.

The arts of Tai Chi Chuan and the Tao style contain graceful dance-like movements. The origin of these movements can be traced directly to their predecessor, Chi Kung. Whereas the Chi Kung movements were practiced mostly to develop one's chi, the more modern movements of Tai Chi Chuan and the Tao style were adapted for use in combat. One should note that many Chinese words translate into English with the same spelling although their ideographs, and thus their meanings, differ. The word Tao, in this instance, is unrelated to the Tao of ''the

Way.'' Likewise, the Yang style of Tai Chi Chuan derives its name from Yang Chan Po, its founder, and has no hidden meaning.

Andrew Lum learned the Yang style from Tung Fu Ling, the son of Tung Ying Kit. Tung Ying Kit was a disciple of Yang Chan Po, who is revered as one of the finest masters of all time. From this lineage Andrew Lum can trace his Tai Chi heritage to one of the founding fathers of modern Tai Chi forms. It is fortunate for Lum that he speaks both Mandarin and Cantonese dialects, for Tung Fu Ling emigrated to Hawaii at a late age and speaks no English. Lum continued his studies with Tung for many years and now, with the permission of his previous master, he teaches both the Tao and Yang styles.

Andrew Lum's classes are deceptively informal. Several of his advanced students lead small groups through Tai Chi movements. Lum mingles with the clusters of students, stopping to explain, guide, encourage, or to ask a student about the family, a friend, or a new baby. His brown pants and print shirt do little to distinguish him from his students. He needs no formality or special uniform. While casual and unassuming, there can be no mistaking that this is Andrew Lum.

Although all three masters have different methods of conducting their classes, there is something similar about them. This "something" is reflected in the philosophy and attitudes they share. It is the philosophy of good will to all persons. Yamamoto says it this way: "Whatever you do in the world will always come back to you. This is the law of karma. If you do good—always end up good. You do bad—always end up bad. It does not appear immediately; but ultimately it rules your life."

Yamamoto, Siou, and Lum form a unique combination of disciplines, philosophies, and attitudes. While they share a belief in certain principles, it is important to note that there is room for individual interpretation. The three approach many things from differing points of view. As they speak of their divergent arts it will be seen how both their philosophies and interpretations, their similarities and differences, apply to relaxation, physical and mental well-being, and meditation, as well as to conflicts and problems which arise in everyday living. It is useful and instructive to be aware of the variations and divergencies of experience that have nonetheless brought Yamamoto, Siou, and Lum to their present, comparable level of education in the Way. Rather than being repetitive, or redundant, the masters are a refreshing counterpoint to one another.

My approach to *Diary of the Way* was one of discovery. I had chosen my subjects well. Of this I was certain. My duty now would be to observe and explore. I would not try to fit them into any stereotype. This would serve no purpose. On the contrary, because this book deals with real individuals, rather than stereotypes, it offers opportunities to discover the character of each one. It is not an opportunity to be wasted. The master is both myth and legend. He is the mystic, but he is also human and therefore like you and me in many ways. Exactly what is a master? Who is he? These questions can be best answered by an accurate representation of him and his way of life.

In order to capture the many aspects of the master, *Diary of the Way* incorporates two different styles of photography. One is documentary in its approach and shows the master within the framework of his environment. I have often heard someone comment about a photograph, ''That picture captures the *real* him.'' Or conversely: ''It doesn't capture the *real* him.'' The truth is that both photographs are the *real* him. We are many things. And it would be a sad state of affairs if all the complexities of a human being could be captured in a single frame of film! With this in mind I attempted to catch the flavor of each master's life-style, and to reveal different aspects of their personalities. One such picture is of Yamamoto doing his morning exercises in his living room.

The other style of photography is metaphorical. Rather than document an event I commented on some aspect of the master. The first photograph of Yamamoto's section is a picture of this type. It shows Yamamoto as three figures merging. Closer inspection reveals that the torsos of Yamamoto's bodies are missing. Symbolically, we see the master: he is everywhere and yet, when you reach to grasp him, he is not there at all.

Another use of this metaphorical style is to isolate a particular happening and remove it from all irrelevant information, so it may be seen more clearly. An example of such a happening is Yamamoto performing an Aikido throw, Lily Siou doing the Peach Blossom forms, or Andrew Lum practicing ''push hands.'' These photographs were taken in my studio against a plain paper backdrop. By removing these events from their usual environment it is possible to study them as entities, without distractions of any kind. In the sense that each event did actually take place in front of my camera, these photographs also are documentary in nature. But from the point of view that the happening no longer takes place in its usual environment, a distinction can be made.

My original concept for the text to *Diary of the*

Way was that it should emanate entirely from the masters. I began interviews with each of them, while also taking notes in their classes. After several months of editing the interviews and class notes, it became evident that something was amiss. The masters could explain their philosophies, their arts, and share their experiences. But they could not do one very important thing: observe themselves. After all, *Diary of the Way* is not only concerned with the various arts, it is about the masters. And so I decided to add my observations of the masters where I felt it would be useful. Throughout the book, my comments are set in this light, sans-serif type. The masters' words are in **bold face, like this.**

Another decision concerning the editing of the interviews was to retain the syntax and manner of speaking peculiar to each master. If a master speaks in a certain way, then that's the way he should speak in text. In the case of Andrew Lum this means very little. But for Lily Siou and Yamamoto, whose native tongues are not English, the decision had certain implications. It meant that I would not correct any improper usage or nonstandard English. It might be argued that it is of no value to preserve the manner in which the masters speak if their English is imperfect. But, again, this is a book about the masters themselves, not only about their ideas. For this reason I believe it is valuable to convey to the reader what it is like to sit down and chat with each master. Through the use of photographs, text, and commentary, *Diary of the Way* strives to portray each master as clearly and as accurately as possible.

Diaries are thought to be a record of personal experiences and observations, often including one's significant thoughts and those things worth remembering. *Diary of the Way* is not a daily journal of any of the three masters. It is a diary about their way of life. *Diary of the Way* has evolved from the philosophies, observations, and experiences of three unique invividuals. It is my sincere hope that I have presented them faithfully and that readers of this book will come to understand their way of life.
Ira Lerner
Honolulu, Hawaii

Yukiso Yamamoto

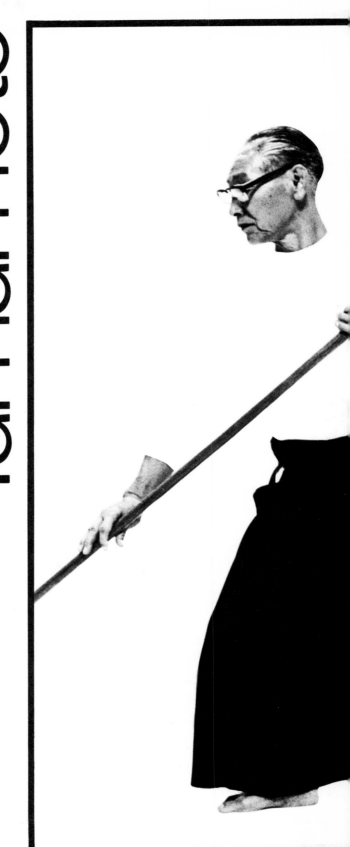

The term martial arts refers to an Oriental phenomenon which combines great personal discipline and spiritual awareness with combat skills. The original martial arts involved many systems of bare-handed combat. Certain systems concentrated on using hitting and kicking techniques, while other systems were based on the concept of lifting your opponent off the ground and throwing him onto his back. In addition to these methods of self-defense, many systems employing spears, bow and arrow, swords, and other exotic weaponry were developed as part of these arts.

The word "martial," meaning warlike, is derived from Mars, the god of war in Roman mythology. This designation is at best incomplete, and perhaps has hindered the understanding of many of these arts. Yamamoto explains:

Budo is Japanese word for what the West calls martial arts. It has occurred to me that the meaning of this word is long time lost. Budo is actually two words: *bu* and *do*. Bu is made from two characters. The first character means "to stop," second character is symbol for the spear. So we have "to stop the spear." The word do comes from the Chinese word Tao. Tao means "the way"; so budo means "the way to stop the spear," or "the way to keep the peace." These arts were not to fight, no...but to keep the peace. You see, Tao means not just the way, like the way you do something, no. The meaning has to do with the way to lead a spiritual life and to true enlightenment. In old times the student would learn the arts not to hurt others, but to develop mind and body unification, and attain a higher level of awareness.

Budo encompassed all original martial arts, one of which is Aikido. I think true meaning of Aikido is very beautiful. *Ai* means harmonious or being in harmony. *Ki* [chi in Chinese] is your spirit and life-energy force. So we have "harmonious spirit." Ai-ki-do means "the way of spiritual harmony."

Ki is hard to explain literally. Ki composes all things, both living and nonliving. Modern science may say ki is energy; that word may be more easy to understand. Energy you cannot see, but you can put it into action. Science calls this energy; we call it ki. Ki is the very essence of the universe. You are composed of ki. By training you can make use of this ki.

To develop inner ki you must unify mind and body, and become one with the universe. Some people think that mind and body are two separate things. This type of thinking creates problems. Mind and body are within yourself. There is no line between mind and body. Which is mind? Which is body? Body you can see. Mind you cannot see, cannot smell, cannot touch. But you know mind is within you. Originally both are one. But people think they are two different things. Based on this, they try to coordinate two different things. Very hard to do. If you can unify mind and body, then it is easy to be in harmony with rest of nature.

Mind and body are both born from ki. You are born from the ki of the universe through your parents. Then why we have such hard time to make this mind and body one? Probably it was not as hard to do thousands of years ago. But now, especially for those in the cities, it is understandable to feel separate from the universe. Modern society does not stress oneness with the universe and the universe says nothing to us.

The ki of the universe only acts, never speaks. So, many people have lost touch completely with ki. Although universe does not speak to us directly, we can learn by observing its ways. Then, through certain training and study, we can become one with the ki of the universe. The movements of Aikido are designed to put us back in touch with the natural laws of ki.

When first learning Aikido movements I thought, "Oh yes, now I must move this way." But gradually I stopped conscious thought. I just moved, my mind and body together. When you ride in elevator to bottom floor, no doubt your body goes down. But sometimes your mind goes up! No, you must go together. How to do it?

Within yourself you have one point which is the center of you. It is your center of gravity. We call this your *one point.* To become one with the universe you must imagine that the universe itself is concentrated inside your one point. To do this, I concentrate. I keep dividing the universe in half until it is infinitely small. I just think, "Smaller, smaller, half, half, half, half, half...." Concentrating, I bring the entire universe to my one point, to one microscopic point. Now I am one with the universe.

Next I practice expansion. I imagine ki of the universe flowing out from my one point, traveling forever in all directions. I extend into space. Now I am centered. Space is limitless; it has a limitless radius. Because of this, no matter where I stay I am always center of universe. If I move one hundred feet to the left, I am still in the center! So no matter where I go—up, down, side, or like this—I am always in center of universe.

The result of Yamamoto's expansion-and-contraction technique is both aesthetic and practical. Aesthetically he develops a profound sense of oneness with the universe. It is his ability to see himself as united with it in a positive way which reinforces his love for all things. By acknowledging the universe, something many times more vast than himself, Yamamoto does away with the conceit which causes selfishness.

The physical effect of expansion and contraction is an acute awareness of one's center of gravity. "Keeping one point" or being "centered" are Aikido terms for a state of consciousness in which one feels united with the entire universe and is at the same time completely aware of one's bodily relationship to the universe. Suppose a master were seated on a bench and that bench suddenly collapsed. The master, being centered, would be so aware of his bodily relationship with the bench, and so aware of his or her center of gravity, that as the bench began to collapse the master would still maintain his balance and would not fall to the ground. Part of the explanation for this seemingly magical feat is that a master of Aikido does not make himself wholly dependent for support upon the chair in which he sits. The master would not fall over the loose railing of a bridge either, for he would not make himself dependent upon it for support. Yamamoto says that we should try to "maintain one point" or be "centered" at all times. He then adds that this is impossible to do, but states that being centered for even one minute out of an entire day will add to your awareness and enrich your relationship with the universe.

His black skirt surrounds you!
Do not reach to strike his body;
It is not there.

Yamamoto practices the movements of the wooden staff.

When my students practice the meditation, I test them. They must maintain this concept of being one with the universe. First, they must remain calm and relaxed. Otherwise they will stop flow of ki. They concentrate ki into one point; then let it flow out continuously. Their ki flows out from one point like the rays of sun. They are completely centered in the universe; they are one with it. Now I make test. I press against the chin or shoulder and try to move my student. If she keeps calm and her ki is flowing outward, then it is difficult to move her; she is very strong. If student moves easily usually is one of two reasons. Perhaps the student has tensed her muscles, trying to use physical strength to stop me from moving her. This constriction of the muscles stops the flow of ki. She thinks she is strong, but she is not. Or, perhaps the student has learned that she should not tense her muscles, so she tries to relax completely. Sometimes a student may confuse being "relaxed" with just being limp and soft. She forgets to send out the ki from her one point and can also be easily moved.

When Yamamoto slowly places his hand on each student, he has the possibility of creating physical and emotional stress in each one. He is, after all, the master. As he nears each student, he can sense whether or not his mere presence and the anticipation of his test has already caused the student's mind to waver. Executing the test is simply a formality in these instances. Other students may keep their ki flowing until Yamamoto applies a light amount of pressure, at which time they tense up and stop the flow. Advanced students will stay calm. Yamamoto cannot move them easily. He will try to trick them, and some will fall prey to his deception. Others will not. A large smile fills his face when a student has managed to maintain calmness despite his ploys.

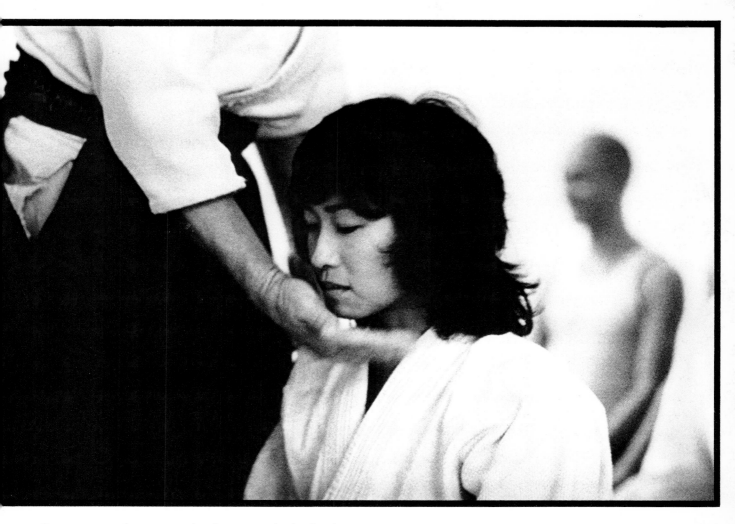

One may stand so strong that he cannot be budged,
And yet move so well that a footprint never shows,
Seal an entrance so tight, though using no lock,
That it cannot be opened,
Bind a hold so firm, though using no cord,
That it cannot be untied.
    Lao-tzu

As Yamamoto achieves a state in which he is at once both calm and energetic, so too does he create another paradox, that of strength and gentleness. Can one be strong and gentle simultaneously? Yamamoto believes so. Kindness is closely related to Yamamoto's concept of gentleness. "Kindness," he says, "is to have a tender heart and good will to all persons." Even as he throws an assailant with *kote gaeshi*, the wrist-twisting throw, Yamamoto's good will is ceaseless. He seems to be helping, almost nursing his opponent. As we look at the opponent, a blur in midair, we have no fear that he will be injured. Something in the master's manner, in his expression, tells us that everything will be all right. One can feel confident that Yamamoto will guide this person to safety. He believes in good will to all persons, including those who would do him harm. This is because of his belief in the law of karma.

Whatever you do in the world will always come back to you. This is the law of karma. If you do good—always end up good. You do bad—always end up bad. It does not appear immediately; but ultimately it rules your life.

Kote-gaeshi, "the wrist-twisting throw."

As a gyroscope spins faster and faster,
Its motion appears more calm.
So it is with the Master,
Whose outward calm is a mass deception
Of the energy he possesses.

The relationship of strength and kindness is suggested in Yamamoto's posture. His hands have a most secure grip on his attacker, but there is no indication of any strain. He performs this action so effortlessly that one must conclude there is something left unexplained, something below the surface which cannot be readily seen. Yamamoto tells us that this "something below the surface" is the flow of ki, the invisible life force.

Another glance at Yamamoto's posture and that of his opponent brings to light the nature of their feelings toward one another. Yamamoto appears to be bowing with humble respect for his attacker, who is after all, his student. Oddly enough, the student also seems to be bowing to Yamamoto—in midair and upside down, but still in a posture quite respectful of his teacher. This upside-down bowing on the part of the student is no doubt a mere coincidence and certainly involuntary. However, it is an appropriate coincidence, because a mutual respect does exist between Yamamoto and his student. In part, it is this mutual respect that teacher and student have for one another which allows a seemingly violent act to become an expression of spiritual harmony and good will.

For those not familiar with Aikido, this question may come to mind: "If Aikido means way of spiritual harmony, then why we throw each other?" Answer to this question is fascinating. Through breathing and meditation we practice keeping one point. This is first step to spiritual harmony, developing mind and body coordination. But is easy to be in spiritual harmony when you are sitting by yourself in quiet places somewhere. Life is not so easy. Always there is the possibility of conflict. We do not sit still in a quiet room all our lives. In Aikido practice we learn to maintain one point and be calm when we are in motion and when conflict arises.

When we are attacked this represent possible conflict. In Aikido we practice avoid the conflict. We never go against the opponent's strength. Rather, we lead the strength away from us. This principle of avoiding conflict can be applied to anything, not only self-defense. However, after you understand how we use this principle in self-defense, it becomes more easy to apply it to your daily living.

When someone tries to hurt an individual, this is going against the natural law of harmony in the universe. If person being attacked fights back with physical strength, then this person also goes against natural law of harmony in universe. If someone attacks you, possibly you might overcome this attack by using your physical strength. But this would only be a short-term victory. Sure, maybe you win this time, but there is always some others who are stronger than you. There is no purpose to compete with individuals. Always there is someone stronger than you. In Aikido we practice "winning without fighting." This is absolute. Avoid the conflict and you always win. If someone tries to punch you, simply move out of the way. This is the simplest example. We look at everything in the positive way in Aikido. When someone attacks you, he gives you a present of his strength. To make use of this gift you must know how to receive it.

When someone hits you, he is extending his ki toward you. His ki starts to flow even before his body moves. It starts when he thinks he will hit you. And before he can hit you he must think he is going to hit you. His actions are directed by his mind. So, we do not need to deal with his body at all if we can redirect his mind and the flow of his ki. This is the secret: lead his mind and ki away from you and his body will naturally follow.

To lead his mind you must not upset the flow of his ki or give him bad feelings. If you touch his body, you do not push or pull or hit. All these give bad feeling. You touch softly and gently in order to lead his mind. His mind thinks, "This feels good," and so his body follows.

To lead his mind you must keep centered, so you will not be thrown off course. Then, try to feel his ki before it reaches you. This is a sensitivity training, to be sensitive to the flow of another's ki. As his ki approaches, you direct your ki to flow in the same direction as his ki intends to go. Now both your ki and his ki are one, flowing in the same direction. Difference is that you are centered and he is not. Since he extend ki with intent to hit you and you let him keep extending ki, he is overextended. Maybe he is trying to regain his centering. Now you can lead his ki and direct it. One very important point to lead the mind is keeping the proper distance. *Ma-ai* is the safe distance between you and another person. With proper ma-ai you can lead someone's mind easily. If you are too close you may be injured. However, if you are too far away you cannot lead his mind.

When an attack comes you must remember to deal with the mind and flow of ki, not with the physical. If you can lead the mind, the body must follow. To do so you must have a strong flow of ki yourself. When your flow of ki is strong, this energy travels out from your center part to your fingers and continues from your fingertips into the universe. We call this extending your ki. One may have such a strong flow of ki that it is not necessary to physically touch your opponent in order to throw him. The ki flowing from your fingertips is sufficient. We call this *kokyu-nage,* "the touchless throw." In this case you lead the opponent only through the flow of your own ki. This is ideal, but not always possible.

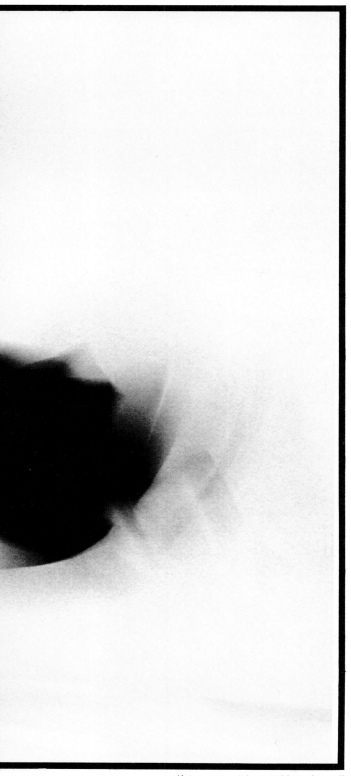

Proper falling technique also follows the Aikido philosophy. We must learn proper falling technique in order to practice Aikido safely. When you are being thrown it is too late to turn back. So you let your body follow the motion of the throw and roll with it. We do a type of shoulder roll in which we roll over a great part of our body and absorb the shock. In doing this we avoid conflict and prevent serious injury to ourselves. There are many fine points of this art, but the principles are always the same. In practicing Aikido we learn whether we are the thrower or the person being thrown. When I throw my students I try to give them a good feeling. From my example they learn not to have bad intentions for others. Also they practice falling, which is a way of avoiding conflict.

I do not practice Aikido for self-defense reasons. I do not think any serious students practice this art for self-defense. The movements are simply a way to visually demonstrate the Aikido principles. These principles of nondissension and avoiding conflicts can be applied to our everyday life. This is the purpose of studying Aikido. If you have love in your heart for all creation, the universe itself is your protector. There is no self-defense for those with ill intentions.

Kokyu-nage, "the touchless throw."

Most important thing I learn from Aikido is breathing and meditation. Breathing and meditation are like roots of a tree. Without roots tree doesn't survive; it dies. In Japanese we call this training *kon,* the root. Very, very essential. If you don't have this breathing and meditation practice you cannot develop your ki very well. This training change my life completely.

One type of meditation is the technique I described earlier in which you become centered in the universe. When doing this meditation, or other kinds, you must use proper breathing methods.

When you breathe you must fill your entire lungs with air. Most people use only top portion of their lungs; they do not fill up the bottom part. If you breathe correctly you will fill up bottom of lungs, as well as the top. Opera singers use this type of breathing. It is no secret; it is the natural way. It is how you breathe automatically when you are asleep. But we have learned so many incorrect ways that when we are conscious we interrupt this natural process with an inferior method. The proper breathing method gives us the most energy with the least amount of work. Once mastered it is effortless.

We are constantly breathing, from the time we are born until the time we die. If we learn to breathe efficiently we will have much more energy to devote to our daily tasks. Early in my judo training I understood this proper breathing. My instructor would ask me to have a judo match with six, maybe seven boys my own age—one after another. I did not have time to rest, yet after one or two minutes with the fifth or sixth boy he would be more tired than me. I don't think my skill at that time was much advanced from my peers. But proper breathing made the difference. They always "Puff, puff, puff!" I was not expending such great amounts of energy because I did the proper breathing. Physically, in this example, one can see the difference proper breathing makes. Although it would be hard to measure a difference in mental power, I believe it exists there also, maybe more so. I am convinced that the powers of mental concentration are greatly increased with proper breathing.

Now, why do you sleep? During daytime you exhaust your life power. You get tired because this power is exhausted. So evening time you sleep and replace this life power. If you do proper breathing your power becomes stronger and you need less sleep. I always do at least one half hour of breathing and meditation exercises before I go to bed. This relaxes my mind and body and makes the sleep more beneficial.

Before I took up proper breathing I get tired all the time. Even though I didn't do too much except wake up, I still get tired. Now that feeling is gone. I feel much pep in the morning. My health in general is so much better! My bedtime is anytime I take a nap. I can take a nap whenever I wish. So, if I feel

"The air we breathe is a most important thing.
It is a gift of love from the universe."

Yamamoto uses wooden blocks to lead class in breathing exercises.

tired, just close my eyes for fifteen minutes of sleep. I don't use any alarm clock either. I put the thought into my subconscious mind. You have to look in mirror and command yourself: "You get up at six o'clock in the morning." That is telling your subconscious mind. Then you sleep. Six o'clock, wake up! When I travel to other islands I don't carry alarm clock, I just get up when I wish. If I want, I can get up at three A.M. I don't look in mirror any more. I just think: three o'clock. This is a long type of training. You are training the subconscious mind.

Your subconscious mind affects how you react to things in your daily life. Since breathing and meditation are to train the subconscious mind, this has profound effect on your outlook in life. Training your mind to wake up at a certain time is a useful training, but the value of breathing and meditation goes much deeper than that.

Breathing and meditation teach us to be one with the ki of the universe and to respect all God's creation. When inhaling you are drawing in the ki of the universe to your one point. This ki unites with your body to give you strength. When exhaling we must feel our own ki pour forth from our one point and reach toward the heavens. This sharing of life energy unites us with the universe.

The air we breathe is a most important thing. It is a gift of love from the universe. We must always be grateful. As we become appreciative of the air we breathe, so too must we learn to appreciate everything in the universe. Through breathing and meditation I have come to believe that I am part of an infinite universe in which all things are united. If you believe that all mankind is united, you will be more considerate of others, for every individual is somehow connected to you through the ki of the universe. This is what breathing and meditation have taught me.

My wife and I have never fought in more than forty-two years of marriage. Maybe we had some harsh words once, but I cannot remember when. We are connected through the ki of the universe. Because we are so close our ki is constantly flowing back and forth to one another. To fight with her would be like fighting with part of myself. This attitude must extend to everyone, not only those close to you. If you hate just one person, it makes it hard to love anyone. When we appreciate all that is around us it makes our love for those close to us even stronger.

Yamamoto uses the meditation bells to strengthen his ki and develop spiritual equanimity. He asserts his inner peace amidst the powerful and clangorous ringing he creates. With each tintinnabulation, Yamamoto chants the rhythmic affirmation: *Toho kami emi tame, toho kami emi tame, toho kami emi tame.* "May all the gods have grace on me."

The clanging and chanting are unrelenting. To what end does this man sit, clad in black skirt, with voice and bell united in a deafening thunder? One might easily conclude he is insane! The esoteric nature of his discipline makes many of his practices curious, to say the least.

Purpose of this training is to remain calm while under stress and to purify your mind and body. We call this practice *misogi*. Originally, the word misogi comes from the Shinto religion and means to go to river and cleanse oneself. We use this word in Aikido for certain breathing and meditation exercises because we believe they have a cleansing effect on the mind and body.

This vigorous chanting and bell ringing requires much flow of ki. The beginner cannot do for more than one or two minutes continuously. With practice you can do for twenty minutes with much power. This power must come from a strong ki developed from mind and body unification. Physical strength will not do. Your arm will be tired immediately because the bell is heavy. Also your throat will become hoarse from continuous chanting. When done with a positive flow of ki and correct breathing, you do not feel any ill effects. Sometimes we practice with twenty, fifty, or one hundred students in a room. The sound of bells is so loud and the flow of ki so great that we say, "Even the four walls will learn Aikido."

"Toho kami emi tame,
    toho kami emi tame,
    toho kami emi tame."
"May all the gods have grace on me."

In ancient times the master of martial arts was expected to be able to defend himself at any given moment. This expectation led to the development of several beautiful and unlikely martial art forms. One is that of the *boken,* a stylized wooden sword. Many of the boken movements are based on the supposition that the master will be forced to defend himself from a seated or kneeling posture. Classically, the master would use this art to defend himself if attacked while having tea. He would not have the time to rise before the assailant's sword cut his throat. And so the master learned to defend himself against two and three attackers without once rising to his feet. Today Yamamoto practices these movements for quite a different reason.

When the boken is used properly it moves through the air so swiftly that one can hear the air being pushed aside. It comes to rest with quiet perfection, devoid of the slightest movement or fluctuation. As Yamamoto uses the boken he maneuvers about on his knees with the grace of an Olympic figure skater dancing on ice. The prerequisites for performing these arts are formidable. Yamamoto tells us that the mind controls the body and that the body is the "mirror of the mind."

Yamamoto, in classic kneeling posture, assumes ''on guard'' position with boken.

The forward thrust.

Pivot to rear corner.   Pivot to forward corner.

When using boken hold it gently, the way a little baby grabs your finger. A baby holds softly but the grip is snug and firm. To learn proper swinging of boken, stand in front of a leaf hanging five feet above the ground. Swing the boken down, just touching the leaf, but without causing it to move. Swing slowly and smoothly. Keep practicing with the boken until you can touch the leaf without moving it. You must come to a complete stop when you touch. Complete stop means mind must stop first. This is just the beginning.

After you know this, swing boken fast, at full speed. Swing and swing. Each time just touch the leaf—just touch.

To move the boken quickly, you must move your mind quickly. It's not the idea to just try swinging boken more quickly. Your mind must move as fast as the boken or you are not in control of the movement. Boken is in control of you in that case. This is not good. We must teach the mind to move swiftly, only then can we train the body to follow.

To stop the boken completely your mind must not be tense. The body is the mirror of the mind. If your mind is tense or wanders, the boken will waver instead of stopping completely. If your mind is calm, the boken will stop without even slightest wavering.

Practicing with the boken gives Yamamoto a means of observing his own progress in mind-and-body coordination, for, as he points out, the degrees of control the student can exercise over the boken are graduated in difficulty.

Next, practice running toward the leaf and swinging. Same thing: just touch! Soon you can run from any distance, swing at full speed, and stop on a pin head. Then your control is good. Now you can hang several leaves from silk thread all around you. Practice with all of them, swinging in all directions: one, two, three, four, five! Just touch each leaf—no movement. This is very advanced.

We believe our spirit enters the boken as we use it. After many years a part of our spirit is actually in it. For this reason we never let just anybody use our boken. Whoever uses it will affect its spiritual energy. So, usually, we let no one use it except ourselves.

Sometimes a teacher will loan his boken to a student in the class. Because the teacher's spirit is in that boken, this is considered an honor. Several years ago my Aikido instructor, Tohei Sensei, gave me his boken. He was visiting Hawaii and just before he left he said, "Yamamoto, you keep this for me." Well, I didn't know what to say to express my feelings. I felt very privileged. This was a very great honor. Of course, he knew how I felt. I have used his boken ever since that day. Even now, so many years later, I know that his spirit is still in that boken.

On guard to the rear.

A journey of ten thousand miles begins with the first step.

Desolation Trail, Volcano National Park, Hawaii.

I find good people good,
And I find bad people good
If I am good enough;
I trust men of their word,
And I trust liars
If I am true enough;
I feel the heartbeats of others
Above my own
If I am enough of a father,
Enough of a son.

    Lao-tzu

The masters of Aikido and other Japanese martial arts are given the title *Sensei*. *Sen* means "before," and *sei* means "born." In Japanese we use this word to mean "teacher." But literal meaning is "one who is born before." The one who is born before you is your teacher. In reality this not always the case. Some people learn faster than others, some slower. It has been said that a person may have ten years of experience, or one year of experience repeated ten times. By this we mean that time alone is not the true indication of how much one has learned. Even so, we still use the word sensei to mean teacher.

In martial arts the title Sensei is Japanese equivalent of master. It is only given to those who are most deserving. By definition, the master is one who teaches. We believe that only those who are exceptional teachers are true masters. After one reaches a certain level in Aikido, only way to substantially further the development is by teaching.

For instance, when I first start teaching my students make all kinds of mistakes. Soon I realize that they just copying me. It is easier to see the mistake in them than in myself. "How did you learn this wrong way?" I used to ask. "Oh, well, I learned it from you!" What can I say?

Through teaching others we find out how little we really know. Student asks a question and you cannot answer it. But moment before, you thought you knew it all. Means you need to do some more studying. When you have to teach someone, you find that you must examine your knowledge much closer. Each student has trouble with different points. You must figure a way to show these trouble points to those who do not comprehend. Each time you can do this successfully the point you teach becomes much better understood by you. It would be quite difficult to reach these understandings without the problem to teach others.

If we want to know what type of teacher a person is, we do not have to study him directly. Simply look at his students. The character and personality of the teacher is always reflected in the students. When I look at my students it's like looking in the mirror. If they don't look too good, something wrong with me.

One difference, I think, between my teaching and teaching in the public schools is the desire of students to learn. In my classes the initiative starts with the students, not me, not the instructor. My students all have the intention to learn before they come to me. This is their attitude: learn, learn, learn. I give certain points. Then let them do. Then I find out the difference between some students and others. I pick out the ones who are a little slow and help them. First, I apply the standard test, but sometimes the slow learner does not comprehend. So then I mention that the mind controls the body. This the student usually understands all right, but sometimes still cannot put into practice. Then I use a more physical explanation. I go up to him and touch his head very softly, applying almost no pressure at all. When I take my hand away his head shakes. This is because his mind is wavering. He is not calm. Maybe he anticipates that I will press hard, so he starts to press back against me. This is a fighting mind. If he pushes against me he is not following the principle of avoid conflict. Maybe he is so worried about whether or not I will be able to move his head that his concentration is upset. Either way his mind is not calm. His mind must learn not to waver just because of slight distraction.

The test itself is not to make them fail. I make test so that they can pass the test. If you ask a student to do certain thing and he fails, you must help him until he pass the test. The test is a learning experience. My purpose is to teach, not to measure how much I have taught. So the test must be a positive feeling. Discouraging is not good testing. Testing is to help them feel the right way. I never say, "You no good." You cannot do that. I let the student complete his move because he doesn't know if it was right or wrong way, but he gains a certain amount of confidence from doing. So, if I stop him, tell him, "This is wrong," it hurts him. That is very bad, even though you are the person who teach. To teach you must respect certain amount of pride of the student. I always respect the student. Instead of saying, "You are doing wrong," I don't say anything

about whether he is doing right or wrong, but "I have a suggestion for you." Then I show the correct way. I don't say this is correction; I just suggest. I give him a positive feeling. If you constantly say, "No, do this way, do that way," even though in a positive way, it is always against the student. Correct by saying, "All right, better, better...," always better. And if he does right or wrong I just look and let go. Then, maybe later in class I watch him and he still does wrong, I say nothing. Maybe I help him in next class. If I watch over his shoulder I make him self-conscious, then he will never get it.

Respect...every teacher must be respectful. Respect the students' efforts and their self-esteem and they will have respect for you. Patience is also very important. Patience and positive attitude. If you don't care, if you have that "I don't care" attitude, students will know right away. So most important, it doesn't make much difference whether you know the actual technique or not. As far as teaching concerned, first thing of all you must have patience, patience. Then you must always be positive, positive, positive. Yes, these are the two major points in teaching.

I remember when I was practicing the calligraphy lesson in the second grade. I was nine. I was sitting in the last row near the wall. By accident I throw the brush back clear to the wall. It touch the wall and make a black line. The teacher called to me, "Yamamoto, how come you did this bad thing." I explain that I didn't do it intentionally; it just happen when I swung my arm. "All right, you no-good boy. You stand in front of class." He slap me and put me in front of the class. After maybe twenty minutes or so he say, "You don't do that any more?" I say, "No." But I didn't like taking punishment when it was just accident. So, when I sat down I dipped my brush full with ink and put it all over the wall! Boy, oh, boy! I really get scolded then; hit, too! Just shows even a child doesn't like to be found guilty when really innocent. This second time I had a good spanking and the teacher took me to the principal of the school. He say, "Yamamoto is no-good boy!" You know, first time I did not do bad intentionally but I get the scolding. So I say, "All right, if that the case I do like this." Just maybe I felt rage, that's all. I was young. I think this story is similar to many.

My grammar-school teacher didn't understand the positive way. He told me, "Yamamoto, you no-good boy," so I listen to him and I am no-good boy. Instead, I put scolding into positive. I say, "You are a good boy! Yeah, good boy. And you stay a good boy if you don't do this." But if you say, "You no-good boy because you did this"—same thing, but two different things. So put into positive. This very important principle, not only in teaching but in all your daily life. Work always in the positive thinking and positive way.

I think many teachers like to fight with student when they do scolding. I think they are angry. Their speaking tone become angry, too. That's no good at all. Teacher and children angry. How can such a teacher make good students? Shouldn't be like that. Must always be calm and think of what is good for the student. If you punish the student, that's okay if he or she will benefit from it. Punishment must be for good of student, not for revenge of teacher, or because teacher is still angry. The teacher is really angry at himself because of his inability to cope with the child. Sometimes a teacher may be angry with himself because he cannot teach a slow learner, other times because he cannot make the child behave. If you understand this you will not take your anger out on the child. I never say, "You are no good!" You cannot do that. No matter how poor a student may be, I never lose my hope that I may make him a good student. I try with all my effort.

Yamamoto left Japan for Hawaii when he was nineteen, rejoining his parents who had emigrated five years earlier in hopes of finding a better life. Although a high-school senior in Japan, he was put back to the third grade because he could not speak English.

He attacked the problem determinedly. He enrolled in a YMCA summer-school course in English and spent as much time as he could with English-speaking children. His Japanese-speaking friends felt this was a betrayal of his heritage, but Yamamoto knew that he must learn to communicate with people in his new environment.

When they put me back into elementary school I was naturally a bit upset at first. Then I realized that I always have the choice to make the best of things. So that's what I did. Some people get bored all the time. Oh, this is boring. That is boring. I have different attitude. If you are bored, you are the one responsible. Boring people are the ones who get bored. We all get bored for some short time now and then, but there is no need to be bored for long. It is possible to change the boring situation and make it interesting. When a teacher asked me to help another student with the lessons, perhaps I was bored with the lesson. Instead, I took the chance to practice my English. The students I tutored would usually correct my pronunciation and grammar. Sometimes it would be difficult to tell who was teaching whom.

There is no need to run outside
For better seeing,
Nor to peer from a window. Rather abide
At the center of your being.
  Lao-tzu

Most subjects in the American schools—mathematics, sciences, and geography—were quite easy for Yamamoto as he had already studied them in Japan. Because he knew what was being said generally about a given subject, it was easy for him to figure out the meanings of new English words. His teacher invariably asked him to tutor his younger classmates, especially in mathematics, a subject in which he excelled.

Many of my classmates wanted me to tutor them in math because I used an abacus and they wanted to learn how to use one also. Most of my teachers in Hawaii let me use the abacus during tests because it was the way I had been taught. Later, when I took accounting at the university, I was also allowed to use the abacus during exams. In fact, I still have the same abacus my parents bought me when I went to school in Japan. I've had it almost sixty years and it's just like new. Using it regularly is what keeps it in good condition. It's the oil from your fingers. It protects the wood and keeps it polished.

Aikido is similar to abacus. One must train regularly to keep in good condition. Used to be when I first started teaching judo and Aikido, everything my students learned came from me. Now these same students come back and teach me. I have a hard time keeping up with them. I try, but I cannot keep up completely. They are always learning some new technique which wasn't even taught when I was younger. I am happy to learn from them. I don't say, "Go away from here. I know it all." If my student can teach me a new technique it makes me proud that I have such a fine student.

One must always be ready to accept a correction, a criticism, or a different point of view. An individual should be glad when an instructor offers criticism. The instructor is trying to help improve that individual. He should be grateful. Even if the criticism is incorrect, the individual should still respect the instructor's intentions.

Don't look to find fault with those who criticize you. I think that this response to criticism is one of the most common. Making less of people does nothing to disprove their observations. For example, someone tells a bricklayer: "The wall you are building is crooked." And the bricklayer's reaction is, "What do you know about walls? I make walls all my life. You can't even mix cement. You never laid a brick in your life, so don't you tell me my wall is crooked."

You see, in this story the bricklayer feels that he can ignore the criticism if he can find enough faults with the critic. But the critic may be incompetent as a bricklayer and still be correct in his observation: the wall is crooked. Is the wall crooked? Only way to know for certain is to take another look at it. If it is crooked the bricklayer should be grateful for the advice. If it is not crooked, he should recognize this and know that the criticism was incorrect. Accepting criticism is difficult for most people because it implies, "You are wrong, you have failed." Rather than be wrong, we can ignore the criticism. Finding faults with the critic is one way to make it easier to dismiss the criticism.

Each criticism must be weighed on its own merits alone. Evaluate the criticism and see if it is correct, regardless of where it came from. You will be the one to profit. You benefit. You improve in everything you do much quicker. It is only human to be imperfect. This truth helps one accept criticism graciously.

When beginners hear about Aikido or Chi Kung they think there are special secrets which they can learn to become instant masters. Long after they have started practice and have been taught the basics they are still waiting to learn the secrets. "How do you do this, Yamamoto? What is your secret?" Accepting criticism is one secret; the other is practice. I learned long time ago that the principles of ki are quite well-known secrets. What not so well-known is practice. You must practice every day. Good instruction and practice is the real secret.

Testing and promotions are a part of Aikido instruction which is often unclear. In Aikido we do not try to create an unwavering and absolutely standard skill level for our instructors. This is not our purpose. Students are promoted for many reasons. Suppose a man starts Aikido at age fifty-seven with no previous experience in body movement. Naturally, it is harder for him to learn Aikido than if he started at age twenty. His body is not in the same physical condition as when he was a youngster. Because of his age he will have to work very hard to achieve the same skill level a younger man would reach with ease. When promotion time comes we look at this man's achievement in relation to his individual circumstance. Maybe his skill is not so great as that of a young black belt, but maybe for his age his accomplishment is greater. Perhaps he is able to teach Aikido extremely well, even though he is hindered by physical limitations. All these things are considered when an individual is promoted to a certain belt rank. Each test and promotion should be for the general good of the student and of Aikido.

When I was in grade school in Japan we were required to keep a diary during summer recess. In September we must present this diary to our teacher for credit in composition and writing. It is similar to the assignment, "What I Did During Summer Vacation," except that we were supposed to keep a record of our events day by day. No one ever did the assignment the way we were supposed to do it. Usually, we make up something at the end of the week for all the days we missed. I would write something like, "I woke up and it was sunny. Then I played outside all day, had dinner and went to bed." Some of my classmates would put off the assignment until the night before school started and then make up anything at all. Whatever they made up was always brief and to the point. My classmates and I always wrote as little as possible. Is this human nature? Or does this mean that we weren't interested in learning? Or that the assignment was a bad idea, since none of the children wanted to do it? I don't know. I really don't know. But I do remember sitting down at the end of the week and making up something to fill the requirement. Something which required as little work as possible. I know that children still do the same today.

Teaching children requires more attention to the teaching method than teaching adults. If a grown woman wishes to learn something, she will learn from an instructor even if the teaching method is crude. A child's discipline is not usually as developed. Children need to be taught in a different manner. In Aikido we don't teach the children the same way we teach the adults. The first thing is to get their interest.

Actually, when you teach any child—three years old; it doesn't matter—you play with him. Just create interest. That's all. How to do it is very hard to tell. All children are different. In the children's classes we do a lot of tumbling and gymnastics. The children like these exercises.

We don't explain anything about ki. Instead, we simply ask them to walk forward and look straight ahead when they walk. Walk, walk straight, look forward. You don't have to tell them to extend the ki when they walk. No. Just tell them: "You please walk forward, forward, looking forward and walk." Very simple. Children are good mimics. They copy exactly what we do. Somehow they pick up the sense of ki subconsciously. That's the way they learn. The idea of ki gets into their subconscious mind. Later, when they are older, we explain this concept. But they have already been practicing it; just didn't know the words for it.

Be diligent when working
And playful when playing.
Many are skilled at their labor,
Too few well-versed at play.

Even when they are ten years old we may not mention extended ki or keep one point. Instead we say: "Just sit down and keep your mind calm. Don't think of anything else. Just sit down like me." Sometimes we let them run around any way they like. They play all around. Then we say: "Okay, now everyone sit down as fast as you can and we see how long you can sit calmly and keep still. No moving." They are practicing one-point but they don't know it. We must approach it in a roundabout way.

We teach them respect and self-discipline. When they enter the school: bow. Bow to the founder of Aikido. Bow to your teacher, bow to each other. At the end of class, thank your teacher, thank each other. This is courtesy and politeness. The children enjoy the bowing and they learn respect at same time. Each child learns to place his slippers

The mind ought sometimes to be diverted
that it may return to better thinking.
Phaedrus

neatly by the mats when he or she enters the training hall. They learn to do things in an orderly manner. With order comes discipline. Discipline means to have good self-control and will power. We practice meditation. Learning this mind-and-body coordination develops self-control. We teach these things without mention. If I said, "Now we are going to learn respect and self-discipline," I think most of the children would not show up to class any more. It sounds rather unappealing and difficult—respect and self-discipline. Maybe I wouldn't even show up to class. Sounds hard to me also!

The easiest way to teach self-discipline is with kindness. When you teach with kindness the children have respect automatically and they try very hard. It is their efforts which develop will power and self-discipline. Kindness is very evasive. What is the kindest thing to do? I do not wish to confuse the issue, but believe me when I say that a good spanking can be the kindest thing in the world!

All living growth is pliant
Until death transfixes it.
Thus men who have hardened are "kin of death,"
And men who stay soft are "kin of life."
  Lao-tzu

Never assume importance and you will never lose it.

The concept of soft and gentle being closely related to strength is a fundamental Aikido principle. Yamamoto's belief in this principle is reinforced in his idea of a healthy mind and body.

In Aikido we learn that there is a strength in softness. When baby is born it has soft body… can move every way. As it gets older, it becomes more stiff and soon cannot move every way. After some years this baby is grown up and it becomes more hard to move. When grown-up, become stiffer and stiffer. Finally old age…there is death, and the body becomes completely stiff. So I think you must keep your body soft. I am seventy-two years old, but my body is soft, more like five. So I think I am far from death. Even though I know I may die tomorrow, my attitude is far from death.

I think mind is similar. There must also be a soft mind. Soft means flexible; you can move and think freely…not a rigid mind which is caught in a rut. If mind moves freely, and body, too, then there can be no such thing as senility. I will be over seventy years when I die, but in many ways I will still be young. Of course, I will be old, too. Young and old at same time. That is good!

When we look back on our lives many things seem obvious. Everything has logic, a pattern, a reason. We can see how we did things and why we arrived at a certain place. Or at least we think we know. Life is not so logical when you are living it. Earlier in life things do not seem so clear. Life is always complex, but in later years we forget the many details of our life. This is what makes it appear so simple. All my life I have taught martial arts. Anyone might say to me that it was my destiny, my calling, the thing I worked at all my years. But my devotion to martial arts began quite unintentionally.

In Japanese high school you had to take either judo or kendo-style fencing. Judo is a bare-handed self-defense and I had seen it practiced when I was in grade school. In kendo they use a *shinai,* an imitation sword of bamboo about a yard long. I didn't know anything about it.

At beginning of freshman year the gym teachers have all students try some judo and some kendo. Then the judo and kendo instructors choose which students they want in their classes. In my case the judo teacher pick me for judo and the kendo teacher pick me for kendo. So now it was for me to make the choice which one I like to study. In kendo they hit each other with the sword. You not supposed to get sore when hit, but if you get hit good it really smarts. You really feel it. When I tried the kendo I thought, "This kendo stuff, it's not for me."

Another reason I think I chose judo was that in kendo you have to wear a face mask for protection. And after you wear it for a time during practice it really stinks! Whew! You perspire all over. I didn't like that. I think these are the main reasons I pick judo.

So back then I made a choice to study judo which had nothing to do with the merits of judo. Now I see that this decision has affected my entire life. As I continued to study judo I discovered that I liked it very much. I also found out that you can get hurt in judo just like in kendo. I was lucky that I had a good instructor. He told us that it's not muscle strength that's important. He taught us to stay relaxed—always stay soft—and have a quick mind. He said to use your mind instead of muscle. He didn't mention the flow of ki, but having studied Aikido now for many years, I think his philosophy was similar. It was this early training which allowed me to recognize the value of Aikido.

After teaching judo for many years I was invited to attend an Aikido demonstration given by Tohei Sensei. He was the prized student of Uyeshiba, the founder of modern Aikido. After he demonstrated many of the arts, he invited me to try my skill against him. So first I tried to move him, but I could not. Then I tried to punch him, with his permission, of course, but he just threw me to the ground like I was nothing. I had never been thrown like that. He didn't seem to strain himself at all!

Well, at that time I was a senior instructor of judo. I was forty-nine and had been teaching judo for about thirty years. "How could this be?" I thought to myself. Tohei Sensei is only in his thirties and I have studied for years. What good is all my studying if judo is worthless against this art? Also I was beginning to have trouble handling the younger black belts. In judo you always have a practice time when the students try to throw one another. The instructor participates in this practice and also throws the students. Of course, if you cannot throw the students they lose their faith in you. It doesn't look too good. I was beginning to have a hard time throwing these younger boys. I thought that this is very bad. What is the point of studying all your life if you cannot do well when you are older? There must be a better way.

Death might appear to be the issue of life,
But those who follow the eternal Way
Do not count the time.

Buddhist cemetery, Hawaii.

It was lucky for me that I met Tohei Sensei at this time. I attended several of his classes and then I decided to become his student. This is how my Aikido learning began. After several years of study I was made an instructor. At first I continued teaching judo; it was part of my life. But after a while I decided to devote my full attention to learning and teaching Aikido.

To those who don't study martial arts a black belt means "expert." But, really, to those of us in the arts the first degree of black belt only indicates a serious student. It means: "I am serious. Now I am ready to learn." Only many years after one has achieved the black belt can one become a true expert. Many people reach the rank of Shodan, the first-degree black belt, and then quit. They want only to obtain the black belt. Those who continue further study because they are interested in the art. They always want to learn. There is no end to it. You can always improve. Mind-and-body coordination has no end, no limit. No matter how high you go, still you can go some more. Many people stop after they reach black belt because now they have something to show for their efforts. My thinking is not on that line. I am not practicing Aikido and ki training just to get promoted. No, not that. I practice for my own sake. For my own goodness I practice this. If I do practice, I know I'm doing a little better every time. Becoming better. If I don't practice or come out to the training hall my

progress will stop. Not only stagnate, but go backward and get much worse. So I have to keep practicing. This is for my own sake.

You cannot be perfect in any learning. Anything you do you cannot be perfect. Maybe nearly perfect—but even that is a very hard stage to reach. Once you start with learning, any line of learning, there's no end to it. The more you do, the more you find out you don't know. To try to be perfect and to think you are already perfect are two different things. Trying to be perfect is all right, but don't think you are already perfect. This can have a bad effect. Every year I see instructors who are more advanced than I am. It is hard to catch even a little of what they know. So how can I say this is enough, this is correct. I cannot say that. It's always the same. When I reach a certain stage there is always the next step, one more step. So until my life ends I keep going, that's all.

How closely you examine the things you do affects how far you can progress. Suppose I don't inspect my boken technique too closely; it looks okay to me. I stop, and boken stops, and I think everything is fine. No movement. But maybe boken moves and I just don't see it. This is because I do not look closely enough at what I am doing. Nothing appears wrong to me, so I never get any better. If I can detect some slight movement, then I have a chance to improve even further. This is the first step. If I do not look closely I limit my progress. Maybe after I see my mistake I am still unable to correct it. At least I have something to work toward. The other way I have no possibility to advance. I believe that those who excel in a certain endeavor have this ability to examine themselves very closely.

The word enlightenment has never been used in Aikido training. If enlightenment means to have enough knowledge or to reach perfection, then we feel that this state cannot be attained. The moment you think, "I have got it," the flow of your own ki stops and you are powerless. "I have reached it," "I am at the top," and so forth; these are expressions we do not use. They express only self-conceit. We talk about being enlightened. This is possible, being on the right path, et cetera. To be enlightened is a constant undertaking. If you stop because you think you have attained complete enlightenment, you have lost it. To stay on the path of enlightenment is a ceaseless effort.

All the years I have taught martial arts I never thought about what my mission in life was. It never occurred to me. Only in the past two or three years did I think about a mission, partly because people have asked me about it. I started thinking: "I have been doing this for a long time, for so many years." Now I firmly believe that my mission in life is to teach martial arts. For a "dumb cluck" like me it takes a long time to figure these things. So maybe it isn't important to know what your mission is. Just follow the call from inside. Do what you feel from within and continue in earnest. Don't worry about reaching your goal in life or fulfilling your mission. It will happen soon enough. There is an old Japanese story which contains a great lesson:

A young boy traveled across Japan to the school of a great and famous swordsman. When he arrived at the school he was given an audience with the founder, who was impressed that this young boy had made such a long journey.

"What do you wish from me?" the master asked.

"I wish to be your student and become the finest swordsman in the land," the boy replied. "How long must I study?"

"Ten years at least," the master answered.

"Ten years is a long time. What if I studied twice as hard as all your other students?"

"Twenty years," replied the master.

"Twenty years! What if I practice unrelentingly, day and night with all my effort?"

"Thirty years," replied the master.

"How is it that each time I say I will work harder you tell me that it will take longer?" the student asked, quite confused by now.

"The answer is clear," said the master. "When there is one eye fixed upon your destination, there is only one eye left with which to find the Way."

Lily Siou

Herbal medicine has been practiced in China for five thousand years. The theories and cosmology on which it is based have led many critics to dismiss it as unscientific. Although its assumptions are at odds with modern Western theories, one should remember that its practical applications have evolved no differently than most Western therapies—through empirical observation, experience, and experimentation. Five thousand years is a substantial amount of time for noting the success or failure of various herbal formulas. Thus, while Chinese explanations may be alien to Western ways of thinking, Chinese techniques for discovering cures do not differ wholly from those of Western science.

Aside from its theories, herbal medicine differs from Western practice in its emphasis on preventive treatment. American doctors are not usually engaged in, or rewarded for, keeping their patients well, but the orthodox Chinese physician is seen as someone who prevents illness, rather than as someone whose only function is to cure it.

We Chinese have always stressed preventive medicine, and this philosophy has been woven into our culture. We don't wait until we are sick to treat a problem. Since the body is in constant use we believe that it needs regular maintenance. Not just food, water, and air, but constant attention to its more subtle needs. Western medicine is oriented more toward curing problems after they arise. This is not enough, although it has its merits because preventive medicine is hardly foolproof. If one breaks a leg skiing, or has a pathological condition that can only be treated surgically, preventive medicine is of little use.

Basically we try to avoid surgery. If one side of a tree is yellow we try not to cut this sick part away. We try to make the green side more green, so that healthy energy will overflow into the sick area. You know, your life is like a lamp filled with oil. The oil is our chi. Chi means the same as the Japanese word, ki. It supplies our life energy, and like the oil our chi is constantly being burned up. In preventive medicine we learn to replenish our supply of chi and keep our lamps full. With this philosophy you don't wait for something to get stiff or swollen, or until you have pain. You nourish the body while it is healthy. This increases the level of your chi. When you get sick, or if you don't keep fit in old age, it is too late. There is not much chi inside to regenerate, and more drastic measures have to be taken. The body must be tuned up regularly and the time to do this is before you are sick.

Lily Siou is a diligent practitioner of preventive medicine. Her daily routine includes breathing, meditation, and Chi Kung exercises which fine-tune the body—as well as special blends of herbal tea and other tonics. In addition, she teaches these and related techniques to her many students.

Herbal medicine is based on the principles of Yin and Yang, the fundamental elements of the universe. Before the creation of heaven and earth, all energy and matter were united in chaos known as the Great Absolute. From the chaos came the separation of energy from matter, followed by the creation of form and substance. Then the light and purer substances rose and formed the heavens; these were designated Yang. And the heavier and coarser sank and produced the earth; these were designated Yin. After separating into heaven and earth, they reunited to form the universe. Thus, Yin and Yang are the fundamental elements from which the universe evolved, and all things are composed of them.

Through the ages many meanings have been attached to Yin and Yang. Yang stands for heaven, sun, day, fire, heat, dryness, light, and related things. Yang tends to rise, expand, and flow upwards. Yin connotes earth, moon, night, water, cold, dampness, and darkness. Yin tends to contract and to flow downward. As heaven, Yang sends fertility in the form of the sun and rain to Yin, the earth. So heaven is to earth as man is to woman. Some qualities no longer relate directly to the original meanings of Yin and Yang, but most can be traced with some logic. Because Yang is expansive and flows upward it has been given a positive designation. Contrasting Yin has a negative connotation. It must be remembered that Yin and Yang are one entity. Both are always present: day changes into night, light into darkness, summer into fall. All happenings in nature and human life are conditioned by these two forces. Neither Yin nor Yang can exist in an absolute state of its own. Yang is linked with man and Yin with woman, but within both sexes there is both Yang and Yin. A man or woman must possess qualities which are both Yin and Yang in order to be in harmony.

In herbal medicine all practices are based on the concept that illness, injury, and disease result from disharmony within the body caused by the imbalance of Yin and Yang elements. Reestablishing this harmony throughout the body restores good health. Chi is said to be of a Yin or Yang nature, and the proper balance of both kinds of chi must be maintained. When a person has an excess of Yang element in the body he needs a Yin herb to calm and balance it, and vice versa.

If you are too hot inside, this is an excess of Yang. Tea made from the leaves of the white lotus will cool you off. It's good for dizziness and sunstroke. So this is a Yin herb; it cools the body and calms down the Yang.

When you have too little Yang in the body you tend to have poor circulation, cold hands, cold feet, or maybe some type of joint problem. For this you need a Yang herb; for instance, the paper-bark tree. We call it the one-thousand-layer tree and it is a spiritual tree in Taoist heritage. The spirit of Lao-tzu is believed to dwell in the one thousand layers. Both the bark and leaves of this tree are used in herbal recipes to supplement the Yang element.

Just as each sex is made of Yin and Yang, a plant also contains both elements. The leaves of a plant may be designated Yin, while the root or some other part is said to be Yang. Even if an herb is considered to be Yang, its preparation can change it into Yin. An herbal prescription is usually made from many different herbs; twenty or thirty is not uncommon. Since the preparation of the herb and its inherent Yin/Yang qualities are equally important, recipes become quite intricate.

Caring for herbs, how they are planted and picked, is very important. If somebody comes into the field and makes loud noises, very rude, fighting or angry, this is not good for the plants. They are very sensitive. We believe tea plants must not be exposed to violent noises and actions or they will taste bitter. Watering must also be very systematic.

Ginseng, the most valued herb of China, is extremely delicate. It does not grow in direct sunlight and takes six to ten years to mature. It has such a delicate nature that it can hardly grow in the same soil two years in succession. At least ten years must pass before a field is used again for ginseng growing. It doesn't grow well on chemical fertilizers either. Decomposed leaves or grass are preferable. An old saying goes: "Ginseng only grows when it hears the footsteps of its grower."

Ginseng is a powerful herb which nourishes and restores the body's chi. Because of this it is good for many illnesses. Some research has indicated that ginseng works on the central nervous system as a strong stimulant and has a prolonged effect on low blood pressure.

Man arises from nature, and gets
along most effectively by collaborating
with nature, rather than
trying to master it.

Grinding eucalyptus leaves in stone mortar.

Herbs can be taken internally or prepared for external use. The milder herbs may be brewed into a tea and taken daily. Salads can also be made. Herbs are used externally to heal infections and rashes or relieve pain. For external use herbs are crushed into powders or blended into ointments.

Because chi nourishes the body and is most potent in living things, little value is placed on chemical compositions derived from herbs. We feel that a chemical formula made from nonliving materials contains little chi and is of questionable value. Although chemical formulas are not believed to contain much chi, they do affect your system. With a chemically produced formula to induce sleeping, you take it and right away you get sleepy. But it's a jolt to your system. Herbal medicine is more gradual in its approach and is only part of a much broader view of health care. You can take herbs for insomnia, but you will not go to sleep right away. You will get better gradually, as your whole body benefits from the herbs, and maybe after several weeks your insomnia goes away. Along with the herbs you need to examine the possible causes of the insomnia, and perhaps take other measures to keep it from returning. It is a very personal philosophy of caring for oneself.

Normally a mortar and pestle made of porcelain or bronze are used to pound the herbs. Instead of these I like to use stones which have been formed by nature. The stones can be found at a riverbed, on a mountain, or at a beach. A rock at the beach has been crashed by the water many millions of times, and to form the right shape of a mortar it must be crashed so many millions of times in the same direction. This is symbolic of the Taoist belief that softness overcomes hardness in the way that water is able to carve a rock. I spend a long time searching for differently shaped rocks to use for grinding various herbs. I must also find rocks to use as pestles. The search is like a lesson in philosophy, a constant reminder of the principles of Chi Kung and how they relate to nature. How we pick the herbs, water them, and even how we chop them contributes to the flow of our own chi. The same is true of preparing the food we eat. In most commercial cooking, large pots are used by one chef. His chi is spread thinly amid mass production. When you cook at home in small pots, lots of your chi can enter those things. This is better.

Does it really matter how many times the ocean waves have crashed against a certain rock? Does it matter if an herb is ground in a store-bought mortar and pestle or in rocks carved by nature? Is our food affected by the amount of chi the cook possesses?

Lily Siou believes the way one does things is very important. Perhaps she is suggesting that one's method is as important as, or even more important than, the end result. The Chinese philosopher Tut-Tut has said, ''To be elated at success and disappointed at failure is to be the child of circumstances; how can such a one be called the master of himself?'' Similarly, this implies that the way one does things is even more important than the success or failure one may encounter.

The realities of
life are most truly seen
in everyday things
and actions.

What one eats is important. When one eats rich food, the body gets tired and the mind becomes very lazy. That's why after eating a heavy meal you don't feel like doing much except sleeping, like a lion after a big feast. Your body is using up its energy to digest the food. Digestion is work for your body. Certain types of food create much work for the body with almost no benefit to your system at all. Perhaps this is why I eat very little when I am busy. When involved in a creative project of some sort, I simply am not hungry. It's not that I consciously fast. I don't believe in fasting; I believe in eating only when I am hungry. The body works naturally and I don't pick certain days to fast in order to cleanse my system. Many persons feel that fasting works for them. I have no reason to criticize it one way or the other, but my own philosophy does not include arbitrary fasting. If I haven't eaten in several days, it's because I am not hungry and it is completely unplanned.

Since I do not function very well if I am full, I eat only about seventy percent of my capacity. I don't think it's a good idea to eat until you are full.

This doesn't mean eating should not be pleasurable, only that it should not be indulged to excess. Although certain people are overweight because of metabolic or hereditary factors, there is no doubt that many others are overweight because of poor eating habits. They eat even if they are not hungry, and they eat more than is necessary.

The problem of overeating has partly to do with the values of a given society. In old Hawaii fatness was a sign of wealth and associated with royalty. It was a status symbol to be fat in that society. In America today we encourage our children to eat. Children learn that it's important to finish what is put in front of them, the reward often being dessert. This conditioning is horrible. It alienates them from the messages of the body at an early age. They eat to please their parents, not because they are hungry. Making dessert a reward is especially bad, because it places undue emphasis on it, making it more sought after. All these things can reinforce overeating. Children do have to be taught to eat what is healthy, even when they refuse these things. But the practices which have flourished with these good intentions should be studied more closely. We should learn to feel proud of ourselves when we eat sparingly.

Being in communication with your body allows you to break free of early eating habits. You see, when you are communicating with your body, you are responsive to the signals it sends about your eating habits. You become aware of any damage being done and you also come to know how much you really need to eat.

I never starve myself or wait until I am dying to eat. I can't appreciate the taste of food if I am too hungry. So I eat before I am famished. One way to help cut down on eating is to remind yourself: "I can always have more later. This is not my last meal." So many people eat as if there's no tomorrow. Sometimes I wonder if this instinct has been inherited from our more primitive ancestors. Snakes, lions, and other animals hunt very hard for their food. When they catch it they don't waste any because they never know where the next meal will come from. Most Americans are better off, and it is not necessary to approach food this way.

Whatever one eats goes into the body and its systems. Just eating any old thing shows a lack of respect and caring for oneself. We should think about this. My own diet is rather personal. I would not suggest it to another individual because everyone has different needs. I eat a lot of fresh fruit and am basically a vegetarian. But I also eat fish and other seafood. If you do follow a certain diet and occasionally you break it, don't feel bad or guilty about it. Feeling guilty about what you eat can do as much damage as a terrible diet.

Although Lily Siou is very deliberate about her personal eating habits and other daily routines, she is careful not to prescribe them for other individuals. "What works well for me will not necessarily work well for someone else," she says. Moreover, the elements of a diet are less important than one's attitude toward food and its consumption. Lily Siou equates proper eating habits with self-respect.

Herbal medicine is only part of the larger subject of Chi Kung, the study of chi. Chi Kung includes acupuncture and the internal disciplines of breathing, meditation, and spiritual development. It also incorporates external disciplines; physical exercises and body movements designed to keep one in harmony with nature. Chi Kung observes the natural laws. It tells us, "Man follows earth, earth follows heaven, heaven follows the Way, the Way follows what is natural."

Originally chi meant "air" or "breath," and was intrinsically related to spiritual energy and the unseen life force. As chi circulates through the body it regulates all bodily functions and protective systems. Both Yin and Yang forms of chi flow through the body along paths called meridians. There are many vital energy points along these meridians where we believe the chi is concentrated. The most important of these points is the *t'an t'ien*, located about one and a half inches below the bellybutton. It is the same as the "one point" in Aikido.

In Chi Kung we learn to realize fully our body's potential; so naturally you improve in everything you do. We learn to utilize all the body's cells and to fully utilize our muscles. Suppose you fall down? In Chi Kung, if you fall your body is like a sponge. You absorb and dissipate the shock. When you have an injury you heal faster than normal because the tissue is alive with chi.

He who is filled with Virtue is like a newborn child.
Wasps and serpents will not sting him.
Wild beasts will not pounce upon him.
His bones are soft, his muscles weak,
But his grip is firm.
His manhood is strong.
He screams all day without becoming hoarse.
This is perfect harmony.
    Lao-tzu

My parents' house has been passed on from my great-great-grandfather. The whole courtyard is filled with peach trees, and when I was young my grandparents used to practice Chi Kung in that garden. This is where my brothers practiced also. I always tried to copy them. I am the only daughter and youngest of eight children. I have great memories of the peach garden. I could play and jump and dance and do whatever I cared to. Sometimes I hid in the peach trees and would not even come down for lunch. My mother came to call me and I would be eating peaches instead. Those days were so happy. In our house each of the chambers was named after a different blossom. I was born in the Peach Blossom Chamber, and when I found this out I think I became partial to peaches. One of my favorite things is to practice Chi Kung in a peach orchard.

When I was six my parents sent me away because of the turmoil in China at that time. I had to go on a long trip by myself so I wouldn't be found. My brother took me to the train station and I did not see my mother again for more than twenty years. All this time I kept myself independent. I never had my mother to care for me or watch over me. I have never been a child; I have always been learning and working.

My teachers always took care of me because I had no one else. But they were not my real parents and they didn't really have to keep me. So I had this great insecurity and was always very well behaved. I had to do well in class, because what if my teacher no longer wants me? You see, in China students are very obedient to the teacher, very respectful. For a child in China a teacher is like a god; students believe that he knows everything. Quite different from here. I always tried to act grown up, so they would respect me. I was very much like an adult.

Sometimes I feel I was thirty when I was born. Now, thirty years later, maybe I can become small again. After I left home I had teachers, but it is not the same as your mother. Your mother takes care of you...sewing clothes for you, preparing your meals, holding you and hugging you. All this I missed.

When you have parents, they never throw you out if you do some bad thing. One time I went with my classmates to steal tomatoes. It was not such a big crime because we were taking tomatoes from the yard of one of the children with us. But his parents didn't know. The tomatoes were green but we ate them, even so. When you are a child you do anything. This was lots of fun and I have missed the opportunity to do more of these mischievous things.

I would like very much to go to kindergarten. I think that this would be a very natural continuation of my life. We all go through cycles. Each person goes from hard cycles to easier cycles, or maybe the reverse. In my life I would like to flow into a very carefree cycle. Many people are struggling for a good job, a house, a car. When they get these things they are still looking for something else. I have my discipline and training, a good job, material things. I do not need any more.

I feel content. So I would like to go backward and get something I never had, my childhood.

Most of knowing my mother is through letter writing. I write to her often. Just a couple of days ago my mother wrote me a letter. She always tells me of her experiences and passes on special herbal formulas that are in our family. With each letter she always includes a new one. Usually there is at least one in the family who is skilled in herbal medicine. She is the one its members go to when they are sick, and she is the one who must train some younger person to take her place. When I was small it was my grandfather, but now my mother passes on his knowledge. Often herbal formulas are given as a reward. In our family, when we graduated high school, college, or got a higher degree, my grandfather passed on special formulas he thought would benefit us. These formulas are even written in family wills so they will be passed along and preserved.

Now I am grown and very busy. Last Friday I came into my acupuncture office and all the patients were in their rooms. It was so quiet I thought no one was there yet. So I said to my student Eric, "Good, they haven't come yet. I can go to the bathroom." Suddenly everyone starts laughing from inside the rooms. Sometimes I wonder if I should be this busy. For instance, I don't have too many close friends. I came from China about six years ago and I don't have any family here. My classmates and old friends are all in China and Hong Kong, so I don't meet with them and talk about old times or about home and things like that. Mostly, I meet with other doctors or therapists, discussing healing and sharing experiences.

I wish I had more time, more time to myself. But as I said, sometimes I don't have enough time to go to the bathroom. I have a dog, two cats, and rabbits at my house. I like to sit and play with them. But it seems my time is so limited. Sometimes I feel that I don't spend enough time with my husband, Calvin; I am so professionally involved. It gets to a point where it is hard to cope with a person who is so involved with her work. Luckily, I have a good husband and he understands me. Still, this is a very personal struggle that I have all the time. All day long I am not at home. I relax by going to the beach whenever I can. Even a short time at the beach is okay. It still feels good to me. If I really need the time for something, then I just steal it from somewhere.

continued. She could not transfer her chi, but at least she could stimulate the flow of chi I had given him. Later that day he became conscious. The doctors were amazed. I was very glad. That was over a year ago and he is fine.

After such an experience it takes a conscious effort to regain chi. It took me three days and nights to get back the chi I gave him. Not three ordinary days and nights; I had to nurse myself back.

Acupuncture and moxabustion were developed to stimulate the chi to an extra-special degree. These techniques are often used when sickness has already befallen a person, but they can also be used for preventive purposes. Acupuncture is the insertion of needles at the meridian points. The effects of the needles are greater than external finger-pressing techniques. Moxabustion is similar in theory, but uses no needles. Instead, herbs are burned, usually on top of sliced ginger root or some other plant. The heat from the burning herbs is passed through the ginger root to the meridian point below. Sometimes small amounts of heat are applied directly. The heat stimulates the points and promotes the flow of chi in places that are crucial to well-being. The points which affect an organ are not obvious to those unfamiliar with the meridians. Because several meridians pass through the feet, moxabustion is often applied there to promote healthy functioning of the kidneys, intestines, and other internal organs.

Sometimes the techniques of acupuncture and moxabustion are combined in what is called "moxapuncture." Here, the burning herbs are placed on the exterior tips of the acupuncture needles and the heat is carried along them to further stimulate the flow of chi.

The acupuncture needles first employed by the ancient physicians were made of stone. As times progressed, needles made of porcelain were introduced. Until the last hundred years or so the acupuncturist used silver and gold needles. Today most needles have a stainless-steel shaft and a head of pure silver. This is the safest, and the silver head is highly conductive of heat and electrical energy, which aids moxapuncture.

Acupuncturists use a method of diagnosis that examines the nature of the patient's total health. From ancient times four kinds of diagnosis have been used: observing, listening, questioning, and the taking of pulses. Observing and listening have to do with examining the patient's chi. This includes the "color" of the chi, its smell, and sound.

It is obvious that only those very well trained in matters of chi would be capable of determining the "color" of the aura, or its smell or sound. A Chinese doctor must have a strong flow of chi or he will be unfit to examine and treat the chi of another. If he does not convey a healthy image himself, few patients will trust his ability.

Surgery has held an ambiguous position in Chinese medicine. Confucian and Taoist beliefs in the sacredness and unity of the body have tended to inhibit its development. Furthermore, the techniques of internal medicine have reduced reliance on surgery as therapy.

Nonetheless, Chinese surgery has an ancient and distinguished history which centers on three eminent practitioners: Yu Fu, Pien Ch'iao, and Hua To. It is recorded that Yu Fu performed a successful heart transplant in 255 B.C. Pien Ch'iao practiced in the second century B.C. and evidently was successful in organ transplants. Hua To, who lived around 190 A.D., was the last of the great surgeons until modern times. It is believed that he wrote several medical texts which have since been lost or destroyed.

The oldest medical book extant is *Nei Ching Su Wen, The Yellow Emperor's Classic of Internal Medicine.* It is believed to have been written between 2697–2597 B.C. by the legendary Yellow Emperor, Huang Ti. Since his existence is questionable, the true authorship of *Nei Ching Su Wen* has been a matter of controversy among historians. Most agree that the original work is at least 3,500 years old, but many feel that it probably was compiled by several authors over a period of time. In 762 A.D., Wang Ping, the most famous commentator on the *Nei Ching,* claimed to have discovered the original text. By combining various existing texts and by adding a commentary, he expanded the work from eighteen to its present twenty-four volumes. *Nei Ching Su Wen* is still studied today in spite of its great age. It describes the techniques of acupuncture, moxabustion, and the theories of herbal medicine in current use. It is regarded as the major reference for the Chinese doctor.

The Yellow Emperor's Classic of Internal Medicine established the theory of the five elements, which has been essential to the practice of Chinese medicine:

Yin and Yang, after reuniting as heaven and earth, subdivided into the elements wood, fire, metal, water, and earth. Man, who is a product of heaven and earth by the interaction of Yin and Yang, also contains these elements. The relationship between the five elements and the human body extends to the practical application of acupuncture and other techniques.

It is believed that the five elements can create and destroy one another. The *Classic of Internal Medicine* explains the conquests of the elements this way: wood brought into contact with metal is felled, metal brought into contact with fire is melted, fire brought into contact with earth is halted, earth brought into contact with wood is penetrated. The elements are said to create one another as follows: wood burns to create fire, fire forms ashes which create earth, earth is compressed and forms metal, metal melts to create the waters, water nourishes plant life and creates wood.

All sickness and disease are classified under one of the five elements, and each organ of the body is said to be controlled by one of them. The duty of the physician is to maintain harmony between the Yin and Yang forces peculiar to each of the five elements, and to correct any imbalances which exist within the body.

Moxabustion: Burning of herbs on ginger root stimulates the vital energy centers.

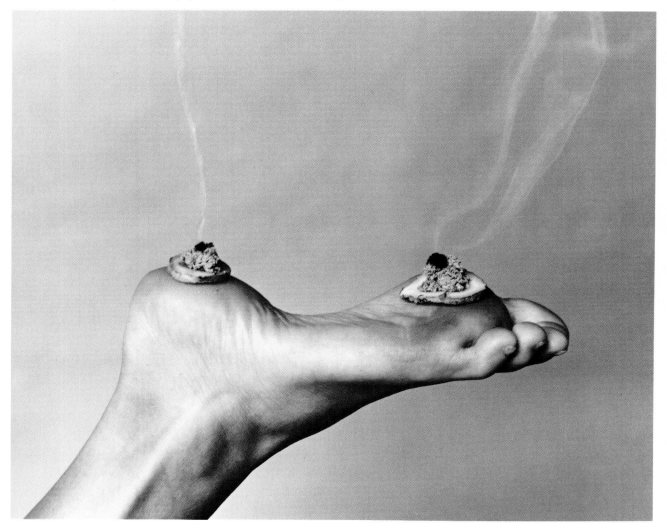

The West has found Chinese medical theory difficult to accept. Critics find its logic elusive if not nonexistent. Chauvinism and resistance to change may have helped to sustain the concepts in the face of modern technology. Yet these circumstances alone cannot explain the continuing practice of an outdated medicine. Although Western science cannot entirely explain how acupuncture and other remedies work, it is clear that to a certain extent they do. Perhaps the reason Chinese medicine has survived the centuries is that it is demonstrably successful.

The natural order of the universe is the Way.
When the forces of the body wander from the Way,
There is discord and illness.
Create harmony, and the body
Is restored to its natural order.

Moxapuncture.

In the range of the Eastern Sea,
There are rocks that look like jade.
They glisten and brighten the four quarters.
They can be made into needles
To cure a thousand illnesses.
Sun Hai Ching

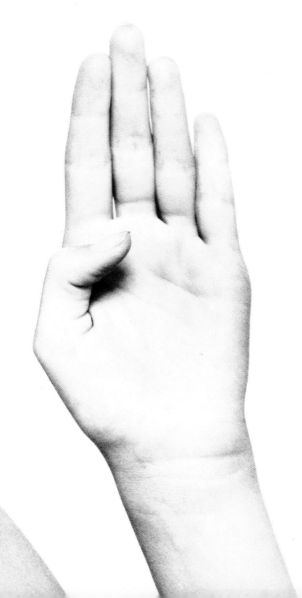

Acupuncture.

In Chi Kung, as in Aikido, we tune up the mind and body together. Both must be maintained. We tune up the body for the most flexibility, starting with the joints. Each joint has its own significance in the proper functioning of the body. We know, for instance, that the tip of the index finger is associated with the forebrain, which includes the cerebral hemispheres; the ring finger correlates to the temple; the little finger relates to problems of the cerebellum, which is the center of coordination and equilibrium. For thousands of years these points have been used successfully to cure illness. We also know that certain exercises stimulate the meridian points as acupuncture does. These tune-up exercises help keep both mind and body healthy. For example, we cannot take out the brain and wash it, but we can exercise the fingers which stimulate the vital points related to the brain.

Take five small marbles and put them in your palm. Now toss them lightly in the air and catch all five on the back of your hand. Maybe you will catch one. If you are flexible you will catch all five. I always do this demonstration for my students several times in a row. Then they try it. It looks easy when I do it, but they never can. Then they learn to tune up their bodies. A year or two later I surprise them by asking everyone to try again. Now many catch three or four marbles. They have become much more flexible.

To begin tuning up my students lie on their stomachs. Now we see if the spine is straight, if the hips are in proper alignment with each other, if the line across the back of the knees matches, if the ankles match up, and so forth. Most people are all out of alignment.

People constantly walk incorrectly, and this causes many problems. To find out if you are walking correctly, all you need do is look at your shoes. Look at several pairs. You will notice that they are worn in almost the same places. If the shoes are worn in certain areas, instead of wearing evenly, you know your weight distribution is incorrect. You are placing too much of your weight on certain parts of your foot. The arch of the foot acts as a shock absorber for the spine, and since we are constantly on our feet, incorrect weight distribution can cause backaches. Flat feet especially cause backaches. When the foot is flat, nothing absorbs the shock as you walk and most of it travels to your spine. A high arch is very beneficial. Since several important meridians run across the bottom of the foot, uneven weight distribution or flat feet can cause other problems for the body.

Chi Kung exercises develop a high degree of resilience within the body. This helps to prevent diseases. When one's system is "tight," it may take two or three weeks to get rid of a cold. If one's body is in tune, its resistance to viruses and bacteria is very strong. If a cold should develop the body will usually recover in two or three days. Tuning up the mind and body teaches one about the self. Lao-tzu has said, "Knowing others is wisdom; knowing the self is enlightenment."

Part of the Chi Kung tune-up is done with movements known as forms. Each form has a theme inspired by nature, and its movements evolve from a symbolic dramatization of that theme. The forms are a moving meditation which promotes spiritual awareness. Each form cultivates a particular aspect of one's physical, mental, and spiritual well-being. Lily Siou tells about one of the most significant forms.

In China, when I first learned the Lotus form, we went to observe lotus growing in a swamp. If you step in, you sink about three feet. I am still only five feet tall, so back then I was so tiny I had better not fall in! The smell of the lotus gives you a very good feeling. It has a light and pleasant aroma, but one that is pervasive and lasting. The wind carries the smell of the leaves and blossom, and it fills your lungs. It is inspiration to be like the flower. When you do the form it is like you are the one blooming. You spread your fingers like each petal of the blossom. Later on you are able to do the form without smelling the flower for real; you can smell it in your mind. It is a good feeling.

The lotus is the summer blossom. Summer is the season of the sun and therefore contains a lot of chi. The lotus draws its chi from the sun and blooms. Enlightenment has to do with the heavens and the primary source, the sun. In Chi Kung the practitioners know that they must gather chi from heaven to become enligtened.

The lotus is a very unusual flower, large and beautiful, but grows in very muddy water. When it blossoms there is no dirt, no mud...only beautiful flowers...so fragrant! Dirt doesn't cling to the lotus. When we were small we used to throw mud on the flower just to watch it roll off. Dirty water rolls off in beads, as if the petals are made of wax. We can learn from this.

We go through muddy water in our life. This should not stop us from blossoming. We can have turmoil, conflict, disappointment, whatever dark muddy things, but still we can blossom. A Chinese proverb says, "He who has tasted the bitterest of bitterness can be a man above men." From this we see that our turmoil and conflict and even our pain have their value. They add to our growth, develop our character, and teach us compassion. We can learn from our "muddy water" if we look into it carefully. Just as the swamp nourishes the lotus, these times can benefit us. From the time we are born many of us see ourselves as victims, helplessly caught in a world where everything seems to be against us. The delicate lotus rising from the swampland is a reminder that we needn't think of ourselves as victims of life.

Each form teaches us valuable lessons about the Way of life. Fables often use animals and animal symbolism to teach a moral. The sly fox, the lazy grasshopper, and others are familiar characters. In the forms we use flowers and plants for much the same purpose. We observe nature. Each flower has some special quality which teaches us about the Way. We relate the symbolism of each flower to our own existence.

From muddy waters
The lotus blossom emerges.
So clean, so beautiful.
How is it that such beauty
Arises from the mud?

Watching Lily Siou perform the Lotus Blossom, one realizes the benefits which accrue to those who practice such forms. As the movements tune up her body they help her prepare for more difficult forms which, in turn, further improve health. The symbolism accentuates the values and ideals which are believed to guide one to the Way. As with most allegories, the symbolism is subjective. Other interpretations are possible. The petals of the lotus blossom, for example, fall softly to the water soon after blooming. One could interpret this as death following enlightenment.

One may ask if doing the forms is necessary to comprehension of their meanings. The belief that the Way cannot be told, expressed by Lao-tzu, is shared by his followers. Words are seen as a hindrance to understanding the Way. They have been called a sickness of the mind, a disease, and a neurosis by various Taoist scholars.

The word "book" is not a book; it is merely b-o-o-k. It symbolizes a book. The real book is that which you have in your hands at this moment. Yet, as the word "book" is read it brings to mind a real book. People learn to communicate through an intricate series of symbols which often are taken for granted. The symbols used in language become a reality of their own. The danger is that one can be very much in touch with the symbols—the words—and very out of touch with the reality the words symbolize. The Taoists tell us that each symbol we use takes us further from the Way. Therefore, it is believed that the true meaning of the forms can only be comprehended by doing them.

The Lotus Blossom is one of the four major forms in Chi Kung. Together with the Bamboo, Plum, and Peach, the forms are called the Blooming of the Four Seasons. The Lotus symbolizes the summer. The Bamboo is autumn, the Plum winter, and the Peach spring. Like the Lotus, each form has its own meaning.

The bamboo keeps its vitality as summer fades and flourishes through the fall, usually blooming in late autumn or early winter. During autumn we prepare for hard times. The Bamboo represents endurance and the ability to cope with adversity. It is very rooted in the ground and also very flexible. We say, "It is better to be like the slender bamboo than the massive oak tree. When the monsoon comes the oak tree snaps in the strong winds. The bamboo simply sways back and forth until the storm has passed." From this we learn the virtue of adaptability through flexibility.

The Plum is a winter form, since the flower blooms in December. Winter symbolizes scarcity. No growing, no harvesting. It is a time to retreat, not a time to cultivate, grow, or plant anything. It is a period of low energy and one must have the energy already stored within. You see, the Lotus Blossom symbolizes summer and is done very slowly because of the heat. As the sun shines down we absorb its energy. We move slowly because of the heat. Since the plum is in winter, we need to move quickly in order to keep warm. This is the principle of Yin and Yang. Winter is Yin, cold, inactive, and damp. We must balance it with a form full of heat and energy. Thus, the Plum Blossom is an active form.

Lotus Blossom form.

Oh, the fragrance!
Though I know not
From where it comes.
 Basho

Peach Blossom form: during winter.

The Peach Blossom form has been one of my favorites ever since I learned it as a child. The peach blooms during the first warm days following a long cold period, and thus announces the coming of spring. The blossoms arrive at the Chinese New Year and are considered good luck.

Chinese legend says that magical fairy peach trees grew in the garden of Hsi Wang-mu, who lived in a beautiful palace in the Kunlun mountains. Her peach trees were said to blossom once in three thousand years and to yield fruit which ripened for the next three thousand years. It is said that the fruit grants immortality to all those who eat it. Till this day the peach has remained a symbol of longevity and has understandably come to mean good fortune and good health, appropriate wishes for the New Year.

The Peach Blossom is a wide-open form with many leaps, jumps, and high kicks. Like the Plum, it is not a quiet movement. It is a very powerful form, mostly Yang movements which can surive the winter.

As the warm weather arrives the peach blossoms quite suddenly. As spring continues many flowers will bloom, but the peach is first. It was preparing all winter long. The blossoming which follows winter is symbolic of the cycles one goes through in life. A person under stress needs to remember that spring always follows winter. The Peach Blossom form points to the value of perseverance and imagination to help one through the difficult periods of life.

Peach blossom on Chinese New Year's Day.

Peach Blossom form: arrival of spring and the New Year.

Praying mantis on lavender orchids.

In their observations of nature the Chinese have not forgotten to take note of insects, and their literature is filled with poems and references to crickets, cicadas, and many other six-legged animals. One of the most fascinating is the praying mantis. Its two front legs resemble a person's hands folded in prayer and the name "mantis," meaning prophet, was given to this insect by the Greeks. Its determination and perseverance are so great that it has been known to cross rivers, mountains, and other obstacles in its search for food. It defends itself successfully against much larger insects, including the cicada. It is so fearless that the Chinese say it will even stretch out its antennae to stop a cart! The poet Lo Hung-hsien, of the Tang dynasty, wrote: "Man's nature is like that of a snake attempting to swallow an elephant; he is never satisfied. In real life, however, the praying mantis leaps upon the cicada."

Interest in the praying mantis is further expressed in the story of Wang Long, a Buddhist monk and student of martial arts. Accounts tell how he chanced to witness the battle between a praying mantis and a cicada of far greater mass. Amazed that the mantis could overcome the cicada, Wang Long decided he should study the insect's fighting technique. After capturing the insect he poked at it with a blade of grass and discovered how it deflects and entangles the oncoming attack. He further studied its ability to counterattack with devious blows. It is said that Wang Long returned to his training hall to defeat his fellow monks in martial-arts practice, and thus founded the Praying Mantis style.

The praying mantis at left lives at the home of Lily Siou. It did not seem at all strange to find this creature on her front-porch steps. Dr. Siou knew that a praying mantis was needed for a photograph. It was quite natural, then, that this friendly mantis should arrive at her doorstep awaiting the occasion. One learns to expect as much from Lily Siou. The day she was photographed collecting herbs, it rained most of the morning on the way to the country. Rain was predicted all day. But no one was worried, least of all Dr. Siou. The rain conveniently stopped whenever a photograph was needed. Her life is filled with such coincidences. Jung would call them meaningful coincidences, unexplainable but purposeful. Yamamoto might resolve this mystery in terms of karma.

Ribbon Dance: The movement of the ribbons is controlled from within, directed by the unseen life force.

The Ribbon Dance has a heritage in the art of Chi Kung, but only in recent years has it been incorporated into formal Chinese theater. Previously it existed as a part of folk culture, more appropriate during celebrations and festivals than on the stage. However, no knowledge of its history is needed to be enthralled by its myriad of shapes and designs.

The silk ribbons vary in length from thirty to forty feet, though they hardly seem that long as they move. Each image the ribbons paint fades quickly as the continuous motion erases its existence. The dancer must move with perfect timing, flawlessly, through intricate patterns as the ribbons carve the air. With all this she must appear to move effortlessly, maintaining the illusion that the ribbons are quite independent and in command of their own motion.

The Ribbon Dance can be seen as a visual manifestation of the flow of chi. As with the boken, the ribbons reflect the internal energy of the dancer. They are extensions of one's arms; but more importantly they are extensions of one's mind. This is why Lily Siou finds the dance so inspiring.

And what of dancers who have never heard of the unseen life force? Do the grace and control of a great ballerina suggest a mastery of chi? Lily Siou believes they do. But like the dancer who receives a standing ovation and then trips over her own feet in the stage wings, we often learn to master certain skills only under very special circumstances. The grace of a dancer may not extend beyond the stage door. Likewise, one may master chi intuitively in some endeavor, but be unable to integrate this knowledge. Chi Kung and related arts study chi consciously, so that we may utilize it throughout our lives.

The cinnamon tree is edible, so it is cut down.
The lacquer tree is useful, so it is slashed.
Everyone knows the usefulness of the useful,
But no one knows the usefulness of the useless.
  Chuang-tzu

The flow of our spiritual energy controls the body, and all things which enter the spirit do, in time, have an effect upon the body. Those things we gather in our spirits eventually show up in our eyes, our faces, and our mannerisms. Each person is born with a unique face. Although it appears we can do nothing to change our faces, they are, in fact, in a constant state of gradual change. This is not only the aging process, but the effect of our spirit upon the body. A plain or ugly face may become beautiful in later years, reflecting the inner peace and spiritual harmony of the individual. A beautiful face, afflicted with anguish and spiritual unrest for a long period, will also come to display this. The spiritual state can change the face completely.

The eyes, the face, and gestures of people tell us much about their spiritual state. If we look at these closely we come to understand others. However, as we refine our ability to see into the spirit, we must remember not to confuse understanding with prying. We must respect a person's right to privacy. A look that is too piercing can be oppressive. The glance which exposes all weakness and cuts through to the soul is not welcomed. If we have this ability we must use it carefully. Such strength should not be used to tyrannize and manipulate others, but exercised only for a just cause.

"The glance which exposes
all weakness
and cuts through to the soul
is not welcomed."

Just as we place a fine sword in its
protective sheath, so too should we conceal
our strength in the presence of others.

Andrew Lum

In modern societies today we are bombarded with multitudes of information, conflicting ideas, and hosts of solutions to our problems. Amid this confusion it is often difficult to know what to do. In less modern societies, where tradition dictates social decorum, there is less question of what is proper. A way of life is passed on from generation to generation.

Today, more than ever before, man has the ability to choose his life-style and values. This freedom would seem to be a good thing, but we are given so many choices that often we are simply bewildered. Many people have lost direction. Overwhelmed with the freedoms of modern society, they have not the tools or the discipline to make real sense out of this world.

The arts of Tai Chi Chuan and Tao style help us deal with the complexities of life. The arts are not a substitute for worldly pursuits and careers; they are in addition to them. I believe that if all people studied one of the Taoist arts the world would be a better place in which to live. People would be more considerate of one another and would better understand the world and themselves.

When we are for our fellow man we are acting in our own best interest. This is a function of the law of karma, as Yamamoto Sensei has explained. But people do criticize others without knowing the jealousy in their hearts. Students of the arts are taught not to criticize unjustly. Since early times they have been taught: "The mountain does not laugh at the river because it is so lowly, and the river does not ridicule the mountain because it cannot move about."

Although one can read about the philosophy of the arts, true knowledge of it is experiential. How do we know the taste of sugar? Verbal descriptions do not give us the sensation of tasting sugar. To know the taste one must experience it. The philosophy of the arts is not meant to be mused over and intellectualized. It is meant to be experienced, so one may test its principles.

Tai Chi Chuan and the Tao style practiced by Andrew Lum are two separate arts. Tai Chi is said to be a "soft" style, because its movements are passive in nature. Soft movements tend to deflect an opponent's blow and lead his strength away from oneself rather than serve as direct retaliation. The Tao style is said to be "hard," because many of its movements appear to be overtly aggressive. Hard movements are those which usually employ direct methods of striking an opponent.

Although Tai Chi is called soft and Tao hard, both follow many of the same principles. Lily Siou told us that Yin and Yang are a single entity; elements of both are in all things. While Tai Chi is said to be more Yin, and Tao more Yang, both elements are present in each, just as man and woman also possess both elements. Therefore, the terms hard or soft are a matter of emphasis, not of basic philosophical differences. Andrew Lum sees the two arts as complementing one another as do Yin and Yang.

The fluid movements of the Tai Chi and Tao styles are practiced in forms similar in many ways to Chi Kung. As with Chi Kung, they are inspired by nature, and a movement is often described by a poetic metaphor such as "grasping the bird's tail," "snake descending to grass," or "the stork spreads its wings." Both styles have exercises in which two students practice together. Andrew Lum tells about one of these:

"Sticking hands" is a part of the Tao style. The name describes an exercise in which one's hands seem to stick to those of the partner. We deflect his blow and maintain light contact with it as his hand retreats. In this training we learn to interpret the unconscious messages his hand telegraphs to us. The way in which a hand retreats can signal a shift of body weight, a change in posture, and/or the probable force of the next punch. It can give a clue to whether the next blow will be an uppercut, a roundhouse swing, a straight thrust, or whatever.

Aside from increasing our ability to interpret these signals, we learn to obscure any we might be sending. We practice intricate punching techniques, so as not to indicate what direction we will come from next. The concealment of our strength is a fundamental idea in the Tai Chi and Tao styles. In the exercise, both partners simultaneously try to interpret the other's signals while each conceals his own. The result is often a continuous warding off of one another's attacks, thus the name "sticking hands."

These arts are immersed in Chinese philosophy, and it is not surprising that they should employ the theory of the five elements. Each of the different striking techniques correlates to one of the elements. Furthermore, each of the blocking and warding-off movements also correlates to one of the five elements. The system is rather ingenious and, as one would guess, a blow designated as wood is deflected with one of the defensive techniques assigned to metal, just as wood is felled when brought into contact with metal. A blow classified as fire is obviously neutralized with a motion designated as water. Logic also exists in the original categorizing of each movement. For example, an uppercut is assigned to wood, since plants grow upward; an open-handed slice to the body resembles an axe, therefore it is metal. Some designations are more obscure. Water is a straightforward thrust because "water rushes in."

Of what importance is it that the Chinese view the entire universe in terms of Yin and Yang? And that Yin and Yang subdivide into the five elements which form all things? How is it that such mythology has been able to produce effective means of medicine and health care, and sophisticated methods of self-defense? Perhaps the greatest asset of this cosmology is that it gives one an aesthetic way to examine life and view all creation. The world is seen in such a way as to resolve all conflict.

Defending against multiple attack.

The possibility of conflict exists when two opposing forces come into proximity. If they are far apart there is no conflict. If they are so close as to join and unite there is also no conflict. The theory of Yin and Yang embodies a philosophy which seeks to explain the incongruities of life and do away with needless conflict. Opposing forces are seen as intrinsically related; all opposites are united. This thought is so powerful, so full of beauty, that its applications are limited only by one's imagination.

It is easy to see that in a world of laser beams and nuclear weapons the practicality of hand-to-hand combat is at least second in importance to the philosophy of living which we can learn from the arts. However, it may be appropriate to look at the practical theories of self-defense. Two reasons to do this are: (1) out of curiosity, to see why they are so effective, and (2) with the hope that a practical application will aid one in understanding how these philosophies may be applied imaginatively to our own way of life. Here is what Andrew Lum tells us:

When you are in a dangerous situation you must never anticipate anything. What if this happens? What if that happens? Nothing has started and you are getting all prepared—for nothing! You must have a calm mind. Anticipation creates fear.

Mark out a path twelve inches wide on the floor and walk across it. No problem. Now lift this path two hundred feet in the air and walk across it. Your anticipation of falling may indeed make you fall. It is the same if two persons come to attack me. I do not say, "I have two persons in front of me; each one has two arms and two legs." In that way I have created eight problems. I have anticipated, and am drawing a negative conclusion that I have more of a chance of being hit.

Here is a typical situation. A person walks up to me with a mad face and automatically I assume he is mad at me. Maybe he is mad at someone else and maybe he is not mad at all. Perhaps this is his natural expression, and with his tone of voice he is an entirely different person. If, before he says anything, I react to his mad face, I have already worsened the situation. I have met him negatively and with a bad attitude. This is the point: if you anticipate an attacker will hit with his right hand, you are not alert to his kick. Never assume. You must be constantly aware. Your mind must grab your body and make it move just so. It is not so much speed as it is perfect harmony.

The fear caused by anticipation creates doubt and lessens judgment. But fear is not necessarily bad. In some ways, fear can be looked upon as a good thing. If there is a little fear, one may be guided to the point of not doing. If you cannot walk a tightrope, fear guides you to the point of not trying it. Fear is part of a message to give a little fair warning. Even fear has its positive value.

When there are several attackers, you must deal with each one in turn. Take the first one coming, not the second. Whoever is closest to me, I will take his invitation first. This is positive thinking. If I have to, I move closer to the first person coming. Now there is less space for the second person to move in.

You must have a simple program. When working with A, you must never move into a position where B will have a chance to hit you. Let us say there are two persons, A and B. You are working with A, so that does not leave much room for B. B is afraid he will hit A and he is holding himself back, looking for an opening. They are no longer working together; they are against one another.

Tai Chi is circular in nature, as is life itself. Suppose you are standing in the center of a large circle, on one small dot. You move around only on this small dot and do not expend much energy doing so. Now A attacks. You must keep A in a larger circle around yourself. Because he must move in this larger circle, he expends more energy than you. Now B attacks. B must be kept outside of A's circle, thus keeping him even further away. Ideally, A will be between you and B. At your central point you need only move eight inches to turn ninety degrees. For A, moving ninety degrees in relation to you may mean moving six feet around the outside of his circle. You clearly have an advantage.

Let me put it this way. A and B plan to work together, but one has to make the first play. Usually, no two events happen simultaneously. One attacks, the other normally is a little slower. You must see your attackers as reaching you one at a time.

Two can waltz together very nicely, but it is hard for three to make a dance.

In reality, this is happening very fast—sometimes in a fraction of a second. With three and four attackers you can still defend yourself, but your margin of error becomes very small—almost no room for even the slightest error. With more attackers it becomes a different story. It is still possible, but the space you have to work in becomes much more a part of your plan.

Andrew Lum says that in modern societies freedom would seem to be a good thing, but that a lack of discipline may be partially to blame for some people's inability to cope with it. The theory of Yin and Yang states that harmony exists when the opposites of the world work to complement one another instead of struggling against one another. Not only that, both are most useful when brought into proper relationship with one another. An excess of freedom can create confusion and incoherence. An excess of discipline stifles spontaneity and creativity. Only as a painter masters the techniques of his art—color, form, composition, etc.—is he truly free to express his deepest emotions. Only as people study their field of endeavor and acquire an understanding of it can they make quick and accurate judgments freely.

The concept of freedom and discipline affects all persons. Many do not see the affinity between these opposites, and within these individuals the two are constantly struggling. This needn't be. Andrew Lum sees freedom and discipline as necessary to one another. He has mastered the intricacies of his art that he may be free to see its implications for the world around him.

There are two basic ways that our eyes gather information. One is by focusing on specific points. The other is by staring or gazing. When viewing a large painting the eyes roam about the mountains, trees, or whatever, focusing on specific points. This happens very fast and the brain pieces together the information so quickly it is as though everything were being seen at once.

When staring, without focusing on specific points, the entire picture is seen—but not well. Surprisingly, motion is sensed extremely well by this method. Masters of the arts have said, "Look and you see nothing. Look at nothing and you see everything." This has its logic, and today science offers some explanation for the phenomenon. When focusing on a point the eyes must look toward it; we focus with the center of our eyes. Reaction time is slow because the brain wants to interpret what it is seeing, and this takes time. In contrast, motion approaching from either side is sensed by peripheral vision. It does not focus and thus no time is wasted in interpretation. Many animals have very well-developed peripheral vision which helps them detect advancing danger. So to see motion clearly it is better to turn the head slightly away from the oncoming object. Focusing is too slow and supplies more information than needed.

Boxers usually keep their heads at forty-five-degree angles to one another. They might not understand why, but through experience they probably have learned that an approaching punch can be seen more clearly this way. "Look and you see

nothing. Look at nothing and you see everything."

After the eyes have been trained to see without looking, the mind must be further trained or one is likely to be deceived. The movements of the master verify how easily the senses can be misled. It isn't that "the hand is quicker than the eye," it's that the movements of the arts are rather ingenious.

The brain interprets what is seen according to its previous experience. For example, it is learned that objects appear smaller as they move farther away. Certain things are expected to be seen because of conditioning. The master accommodates this anticipation and misdirects the mind. His strength cannot be fought. It is too elusive.

The false master is quite ferocious,
But possesses no real power.
The Master does not make such a show,
But his touch is as heavy as a mountain.
  Chueh Yuan

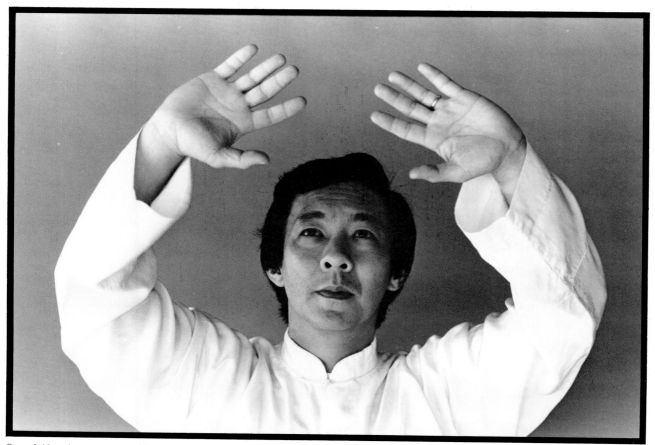

Graceful hand movements of Tai Chi Chuan.

As Yamamoto Sensei has explained, being centered is a spiritual state in which we coordinate mind and body. The *t'an t'ien* (the "one point") and the head are the body's major stabilizing points. Physically, to maintain our balance we focus on the t'an t'ien. Gymnasts and dancers do this intuitively. Try this: standing, raise one foot off the ground. Control your balance by maneuvering the supporting foot.

Next, stand as before, but this time focus all your attention on the t'an t'ien, a point about one and a half inches below the navel. Control your balance by shifting your weight from the t'an t'ien.

Although both methods may prove difficult at first, the second method will prove far superior in time. Attempting to control your balance by maneuvering the supporting foot is like trying to control a lion by seizing his tail. Moving from the t'an t'ien shifts the bulk of your weight. Therefore, controlling this point is the key to being physically centered.

The head is important to physical centering because of the ears, which contain our sense of balance, and also because of the eyes, which help us maintain our spatial orientation. Our body weight tends to follow our head. If we want to change direction quickly, the key is to turn our head. The body will follow.

In general, the body weight should not be divided fifty percent on each foot. The percentage is either sixty to forty, eighty to twenty, or some other uneven combination. However, there are times when the weight is even—starting movements, for example. These positions are for centering. Also, in the process of shifting your weight from one foot to another there is theoretically a point at which your weight is divided equally. But this exists for just a brief moment.

When the weight is divided unevenly you are most flexible. There is one free foot with which to move in any direction. It may appear that uneven weight distribution makes it hard to move the foot that has most of your weight on it. Not really. Don't think of moving the heavy foot. The concept is that you are taking a step with your free foot. The heavy foot is automatically moved and no time has been misspent.

With this flexibility you can change to any position. Like water, we must be able to change to all forms. If a room is filled with water and there is a small hole in the floor, one inch by one inch, all the water will escape. But suppose there is a rock two inches by one inch. It cannot escape; it is trapped. If you are like the water you can escape through even the smallest of openings.

The Tai Chi kick.

The Swordsman is the grand master of illusion:
A magician playing with your mind.
His blade is always present, though not always seen.

In the Tai Chi exercise of "push hands," two persons unite their chi, representing the union of heaven and earth. Touching lightly at the hands or specific parts of the arms, the two move back and forth in circular motions. One of the two is the leader and initiates the first movement; his partner follows. Each takes his turn as leader, setting the rhythm and pace of the motion. Their aim is to maintain an ever-so-soft contact with one another as they vary the speed and direction of their movements. As the leader makes changes his partner must try not to lose contact with, or push against, his hands, whether they accelerate or slow down. Andrew Lum explains further:

In "push hands" we learn to move in harmony with whatever force approaches us. Losing contact with our partner's hand allows it to strike us. Pushing against his hand overextends us and we can be easily led off balance. The "push-hands" technique teaches one to ward off an oncoming attack and still maintain centering. Overreacting or underreacting can cause one to lose it. When problems arise in life we must also remain centered. In this way we deal with them most effectively. But instead of diverting problems we often wait until they hit us in the face. When a problem arises, don't fight with it or try to deny it. Accept it and acknowledge it. Problems tend to disrupt our equilibrium, but we must learn to deflect their force while keeping centered. It has been said that one must "fight fire with fire." This is the wrong attitude. Fire with fire only builds more fire. In Tai Chi we might say, "Fight fire with water." This is a much better policy. Accept the blaze instead of fighting with it. Then gently put it out.

In "push hands" one must respect the intentions of another, so that two may move in unison. But in real life how can we respect those who harbor ill will against us and would cause us harm? To answer this one must examine the meaning of respect. "Respect" comes from the Latin root *specio,* meaning "look," and the prefix *re,* meaning "back" or "again." Respect has to do with "looking again." Intrinsic in the word is the notion of examining things more closely. The greatest respect one can have for something is to see it clearly and accurately.

To see clearly one must not be afraid of looking. But for many there is a fear of seeing. This fear sometimes arises from the desire to remain the same. We are constantly trying to make sense of this world, and new knowledge can contradict conclusions we have carefully drawn about the nature of life, as well as interfere with our self-image. After all, if each new piece of information contradicted the one before it we would be a mass of confusion. People usually form their conclusions early in life and prefer to stick with them, seeing mostly that which reinforces these already formed views. This can mean incomplete seeing, especially if these early conclusions are incorrect. Change is work. It is easier not to change. Therefore, there is a tendency to by-pass those things which lead to the conclusion that we should change. Why upset the applecart? The philosopher Bertrand Russell was aware of the relationship of fear and seeing when he wrote: "Thought looks into the pit of hell and is not afraid. Thought is great and swift and free, the light of the world and the chief glory of man."

Seeing clearly requires respect and great courage.

"Instead of diverting problems, we often wait until they hit us in the face."

Beginning "push hands."

"Push hands" in motion.

Two become one.

126

At Kapiolani Park.

With wife Teresa and daughter Annette.

Raising a child is the responsibility of both parents. When Terrance, my oldest boy, started his second year of school, my wife and I went to his school orientation together. I believe it is very important for both parents to participate in their children's education. At orientation, teachers introduce themselves and talk a little about the subjects they teach. They tell you what to expect, and by meeting the teachers we can better understand problems that arise during the year.

Terrance and Greyson have different personalities. Greyson, my younger boy, is more active and always on the go. Terrance is more quiet and serious. In school their study habits will not be the same, and I imagine that later in life they will continue to be different. All children in a family are different and it is important for parents not to compare them to one another. When you look at your fingers you can see that no two are the same length; this is not bad.

We must see our children for what they are, but must also be careful not to sum them up or classify them. Sometimes we do this unknowingly. It can be very subtle and can create a self-fulfilling prophecy. Children react to what is expected of them, and sometimes parents reinforce or encourage bad behavior simply because they come to expect it. Children can sense what we expect of them no matter how we try to hide it. Therefore, we owe it to them to expect good things. These expectations are a vote of confidence and encouragement. Most of us never use our full potential, and one should remember that, with proper encouragement, a little ability is likely to go farther than great aptitude with no encouragement. If we expect little from an individual, that is what we are likely to get. But if we expect more, perhaps he will try to meet these expectations.

When children are born things they can hold onto give them a feeling of security. Babies are often reluctant to let go of their blankets, bottles, or other possessions. Sharing is something they will learn later. As parents this is one of the things we must teach them. You never find a successful person in life who just keeps, keeps, keeps. That is obsession. Life is Yin and Yang, giving and receiving. A successful person is one who gives—not just in the material sense—but gives of his heart and spirit. It is very important to learn to share.

Although there is no exact model that I intend my children to be, I would like to guide them to be considerate and humble. I want them to be respectful of others and also to be respected themselves. People can be respected out of fear or out of sincere appreciation. I would like them to be appreciated. To teach them to be considerate I must be considerate. Their learning is through copying other people, so I must set a good example. What a child learns in youth stays with him the rest of his life.

A child is not born with the secret of how to live. It is the parent's responsibility to teach these things. A child must be taught to take care of himself and look after his own best interest. This in itself can be a quite tricky thing. Often we don't really know

Terrance and Greyson.

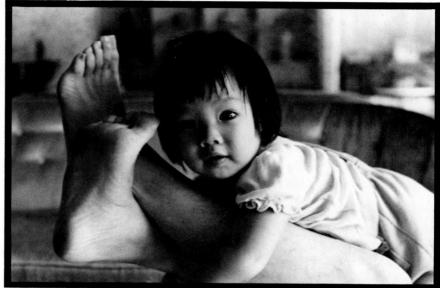

If there is righteousness in the heart,
There will be beauty in the character.
If there is beauty in the character,
There will be harmony in the family home.
If there is harmony in the home,
There will be order in the nation.
When there is order in the nation,
There will be peace in the world.

what is in our true best interest. Anyway, isn't it rather selfish just to look after ourselves? In truth, looking after your own best interest is quite the opposite of self-indulgence. Self-indulgence means to satisfy only an isolated part of you. Taking care of your whole self includes your responsibilities and obligations to the outside world. It means taking care of the entire self—its feelings and concerns. So, if we are in doubt as to what is really in our best interest, we should ask ourselves: "Is this truly for my whole self? Or is this in some way against that which I want for my entire self?"

Much confusion also exists about love. Sometimes the reasons we choose to love are not good at all, and in these cases I would say the love is not genuine. If a woman needs a man to worship her in order to satisfy her vanity, and that man needs a woman to idolize, which is unaccepting of her totality, the relationship pleases only a narrow self. This does not do justice to either person. It is not what either wants for oneself or for the other person. When we sense that love has a bad motive we must question that love. Love should not be a handicap. We can need another out of weakness, but we can also need another out of strength. To need another in a positive way takes a special kind of strength. This needing enhances both individuals and makes them more, not less. If the love is good it will truly be in your best interest. You will respect your entire self more for loving that other person. And you in turn will respect that other person more for loving you.

The law of karma says that the vibrations we give out return to us. Naturally, we are also affected by the vibrations we pick up from other people. When we are with good people we pick up their karma and it has a good effect upon us. So it's especially important that children be exposed to a good element of people.

Children don't always choose their friends carefully and parents, of course, are concerned with this. If my children were seeing someone I thought was a troublemaker, I wouldn't just say, "He's no good. Don't see him." This creates a large question in their minds: "Why?" This question is so large it could fill up the entire backyard. Instead, I explain my reasons to them so they understand "why" I don't want them to see a certain person.

But what if after I explain my reasons they still want to see a child whom I feel may be a bad influence? In that case, I may try talking with the child to gain more understanding of the situation. After all, this child will not be the total influence on my children. Perhaps my children and I can be a good influence on him. I would rather try to win him over to our side than just cut him off. But it depends on the total situation. If there really is trouble, or the children are hanging around with a bad crowd, then a parent may have to put diplomacy aside and step in abruptly.

We learn from those around us and this is a most important thing. Everyone has his or her own characteristics of good. If you meet one hundred people and learn one good point from each, you have profited one hundred times. If you learn only from yourself the learning will be slow.

"A child is not born with the secret
of how to live. It is the parent's responsibility
to teach these things."

You need not set aside
A special time or place to think.
Rather, in meditation,
Go deeply into your heart.

The Chinese say there are places where enlightened spirits dwell. Masters of the Way have journeyed across continents to perceive the spiritual energy of such places. Practicing the arts is easier at these locations. Movements seem to flow, and one's powers and abilities are greater than usual. Similarly, performing in the great training halls is easier because of the spiritual energy that has accumulated over the years. It is more difficult to train in a new hall because its spiritual energy is low. Many masters must visit it and bless the new hall with their presence. In China, only those who have proved themselves worthy are permitted to practice at spiritually enlightened places.

Haleakala, a great volcano on the Hawaiian island of Maui, is one such place. It rises 10,025 feet and stretches more than thirty-three miles in diameter. Haleakala, a well-chosen name, means House of the Sun. *La* or *ra* is the world used for sun throughout Polynesia. Ra was also the sun god of ancient Egypt, and there is some evidence that the two cultures have been in touch with one another, although the details of this are not completely clear.

Haleakala is associated with Maui, a trickster demigod, for whom the island is named. Hawaiian legend says that Maui climbed the slopes of Haleakala to capture the sun. It seems that Hina, Maui's mother, was deeply troubled by the haste with which the sun crossed the sky. Hina spent her days making kapa, a Polynesian cloth. She pounded the bark of certain trees until the fibers formed a pulp, then pressed this into thin sheets and dried them in the sun. The resulting kapa is used for clothing and decoration.

But each day, by the time Hina had laid out her cloth to dry, the heedless sun had rushed across the sky and gone down to the underworld. Therefore, the cloth, which must be thoroughly dried, had to be gathered up again until the next day. This made Hina very angry.

Maui, determined to catch the sun and make him slow his stride, climbed to the top of Haleakala, where he could observe his path. He noted that the sun first traveled up the eastern slopes of the mountain from the Koolau ridge and then passed directly over the summit. Maui then fashioned a huge net of sennit rope braided from the inner fibers of coconut husk. He waited until nightfall and climbed to the top of Haleakala, hiding among the rocks. At noon the next day, as the sun moved directly overhead, Maui threw his net upward and ensnared the great ball of light. Helplessly entangled, the sun pleaded for his freedom. "You will be freed only if you promise to move more slowly across the sky," said Maui. The sun agreed, and for this Hina and all of Polynesia have been eternally thankful.

Hawaiian history records that Haleakala last erupted in 1750. But unlike an extinct volcano, it is said to be only "resting." It is a mystical place. Large, symmetrical cones rise from the crater floor, surrounded by the sparkle of multicolored cinders and ash. The crater alone is seven miles long and one and a half miles wide. It has long been regarded as a special place.

Certain things we do alone, even if others are present. Viewing Haleakala crater is one of these things. Human company is of no importance. There are other more distinguished guests. Although they do not show themselves plainly, their presence is felt.

The path to Haleakala crater.

The spirits of Haleakala are inescapable. The wind tears across the crater floor, removing all debris, as if keeping house for the sleepy volcano. And yet it can suddenly become very quiet—perhaps too quiet.

Andrew Lum climbs to the top of Haleakala to experience its spiritual energy. He feels very much at ease balancing on the jagged rocks. The air is very good there, very good for practicing Tai Chi. But what is the sensation experienced at the places where the enlightened spirits dwell? Is it like the feeling we sometimes get when visiting the site of some great event, or where a great person is known to have lived? Visiting such places is inspiring. But is that all? Is there something more, something less well understood?

The sensation that is felt atop the crater's rim cannot be denied. It is real. For some it is totally exhilarating, for others more contemplative. Still others find their energy drained by the experience. And for some it is frightening.

On Mount Haleakala.

There is that which is explicable
And that which is inexplicable.
The wise man knows that both are incomprehensible.

When I was young I was told many things about the nature of spirits. I still wonder about these things every now and then. I remember being told that the spirit remains alive even after a person dies. And that it usually takes some time for the spirit to find out that the body is dead. In the meantime it goes about its usual business. Once it discovers that the body has died, the spirit will usually return to it for a last visit. I've heard it said that it is wise to redecorate the departed person's room, so the spirit will not recognize the dwelling if it should return. This makes it easier for the spirit to adjust to its new life. Preparing the spirit for its new life is important. In fact, in South China graves are sometimes constructed in the shape of long armchairs, so that the spirit may recline in them peacefully.

It was explained to me some time ago that during the night our spirits travel, and because of this one must never draw upon a person's face—with crayon or the like—while that person is sleeping. If one does, the spirit might not recognize the face when it returns from travel. Instead of reentering the body, it will wander about aimlessly in search of its owner.

Have you ever thought you heard your name being called very faintly, off in the distance, but when you turned your head no one was there?

Some believe that evil spirits attract our attention this way. Calling…calling…softly calling. Answering such a call can be very dangerous because as we reply we are communicating with an evil force and our attention is focused where it should not be. We have thus been tricked into acknowledging an evil spirit, and this acknowledgment tends to increase the spirit's power.

I have studied the nature of spiritual energy for many years, but there is so much one can never understand. Although the stories I have told seem nothing more than folk tales, I hesitate to challenge them. I would never draw upon a person's face while he is asleep. And when my name is called, I am attentive. I do not answer until I am certain whom I am answering.

Andrew Lum practices with Tai Chi knife.

There is nothing more fluid, more yielding than water,
Yet it erodes the rigid strength
Which cannot withstand it.
In this way the supple can overcome the stiff,
The humble prevail against the arrogant.

Lao-tzu

Andrew Lum, Lily Siou, and Yukiso Yamamoto believe their spirits enter the objects they use, especially those used for spiritual training. This is true of Yamamoto's boken, Lily Siou's acupuncture needles, and also of the Tai Chi knife used by Andrew Lum.

The impressive size of the Tai Chi knife tends to arouse concern as to whether it is named correctly. Nevertheless it is designated as a knife, the term sword being reserved for its narrow, double-edged counterpart.

Knife techniques involve twirling motions to confuse and slicing motions to attack. The knife is made of rigid steel, but moves gracefully, slicing with severe sharpness. Using the knife teaches one to move with sureness. There is no room for indecision. One does not "chop" with the knife. The movements are smooth and definite. This requires positive thinking and a positive state of mind which develops with serious study.

The nature of positive thinking should be well understood. It is not simply telling yourself, "I can do it," if something deep inside knows you can't. Effective, positive thinking comes only as a result of correct preparation. It would be foolish to approach a master swordsman armed only with positive thinking. The facade of positive thinking will vanish quickly when faced with reality, because the inner self will know it is not prepared. A mind that thinks it can accomplish anything simply because it wants to is conceited and arrogant. Each of us has limits. We should not set those limits, but rather find out what they are through experimentation and perseverance. In other words, don't limit yourself, but do find out what you are capable of. Knowing your capabilities helps develop positive thinking.

Today many people find almost no time to relax. They are always on the go; too busy even to attend to their own problems. Meditation is one way to rest the mind. It is a guiding point to help us in our daily living. One need not meditate at any special time of day or for a certain amount of time. Even one or two minutes each day can be helpful.

When we talk about meditation we don't mean thinking about our problems; that is thought. In meditation we try to clear our minds. The method is rather indirect. Our minds are always working and sometimes our conscious thought interrupts or blocks an important thinking process. Many persons have tried to remember the name of a place or some fact only to give up after several minutes of strained thought. Then, sometime later, the answer just pops into their head. The mind was still at work, and without conscious interference it was able to work more effectively. This is the idea behind meditation. Don't worry about consciously solving a problem. Your mind knows more than you think it does. Just relax and give it an opportunity to work freely.

This is difficult at first and requires a certain amount of faith. It is paradoxical in that one must think without thinking. The different methods of meditation are countless. Yamamoto described one type in which you imagine the ki of the universe flowing out from your one point. Sometimes a visual image helps. Zen Buddhists say, "Think of flowing water," "a mountain stream," or "clouds." Reflecting upon the beauty of the world can help put things in their proper perspective. There is also the Indian method in which a special word, a mantra, is repeated over and over again. All of these are designed to relax the mind and free it of extraneous thought.

Each morning when I awake I sit by myself for fifteen or twenty minutes in meditation. Meditation can help regulate one's life so that everyday living does not create undue pressures. Sometimes, if I have the time, I take a morning walk. There are beautiful trees in my neighborhood and they give me a good feeling.

It's always good to have some kind of routine. The mind and body need regularity. For instance, if we shift from a daytime schedule to a nighttime schedule it takes several days for us to adjust completely, even though we may not realize it. During this adjustment period we are functioning at below our normal capacity. If we are in good mental and physical shape we can take these strains, but it is not a good idea to be constantly without regularity.

Meditating at Seven Sacred Pools, Hana, Maui.

The body must have a rhythm, a cycle. There is a creative force which exists in rhythm. When a person walks, the arms swing back and forth in a natural rhythm. The importance of rhythm seems obvious in music. It must have rhythm to be successful. There must be a balance between the fluidity and stillness of the music—but it does not end there. The earth, sun, and moon travel together with a definite rhythm. All nature has a rhythm to it. When military troops travel over bridges, the commander has them break cadence so that the force of the rhythmic marching does not break the bridge. This is the power of rhythm. Tai Chi, Aikido, and Chi Kung all deal with rhythm. When our body has a rhythm it becomes much stronger. Meditation can create a rhythm in our lives.

With rhythm and regularity also comes the possibility of boredom. Too much routine is monotonous. Likewise, complete lack of regularity creates anxiety, tension, and unrest. An excess of either is undesirable. The idea is to have both change and constancy present in our lives at once.

The arts teach us that Yin and Yang are one entity. Similarly, all other opposites can also be seen as united. The close relationship of change and constancy can be more fully appreciated when we note that perhaps the most constant thing in the universe is change. Of all the things which may fail us, change will not. It is the most regular thing in the universe.

No matter what, things will change. Of course, they will also remain the same.

The mind of a perfect man is like a mirror.
It grasps nothing. It expects nothing.
It reflects but does not hold.
Therefore the perfect man
Can act without effort.
    Chuang-tzu

Applause: Andrew Lum and students end the day's lesson.

There are some basic differences in teaching today as compared with the old style of teaching in the orient. The old style was very strict...with physical punishment. The teacher's word was law. The teacher or master was the major or possibly the only influence in one's formal education. He was everything. Nowadays we realize there are many approaches to the same problem. We cannot do things in the old way in which you get hit on the head with a bamboo stick if you don't listen. Today we learn from newspapers, magazines, TV, radio, many teachers, and so forth. A student in my class may be better versed in many subjects than I am. One can no longer assume that he is teaching everything. As a teacher I don't like to separate myself from the students by placing myself above them. I treat them as equals and they treat me as an equal. Once you have a separation of student and teacher there is no meaning to the relationship at all. It is not the way things are in real life and it creates an artificial situation. When students and teacher relate as equals there is an exchange of ideas; both of you increase. A good student-teacher relationship is essential.

The old way was one-track: don't answer back! A teacher can go down a wrong road also. Times change. What worked in the past does not necessarily work today.

At the end of my class we applaud one another. This shows our mutual appreciation. We all did a fine job, we all practiced well. The students thank me and I thank them—just like bowing to one another.

But Andrew Lum's class does not bow and it is curious that the class ending is so untraditional. It is very Western. In fact, applauding is the usual ending for most classical and modern dance classes. However curious, it is also fitting that Lum combines this modern closing with the ancient arts.

Andrew Lum has studied the wisdom of the orient and found it useful today. He sees no conflict between the Tai Chi concepts of centering and the laws of physics. He believes that the law of karma is quite appropriate in raising his children. Andrew Lum, Chinese by descent and American by birth, has blended both cultures into his daily living. His class, like the rest of his life, reflects this union.

Yukiso Yamamoto and Lily Siou have also found their philosophies compatible with modern-day living. However, one need not master Aikido throws or acupuncture techniques to follow the Way of life. The Way is a method, a style of living that can be pursued by anyone. In ancient times, masters of the Way studied a wide range of disciplines, including painting, poetry, music, and mathematics. Although Yamamoto, Siou, and Lum study different arts, they share a common life-style.

Accordingly, the ideology of each master is not limited to the arts each practices. The natural laws of centering, the concepts of strength and gentleness, the virtues of softness and fluidity, are thoughts which are relevant to many areas of life. And they have a great effect upon the quality of one's life. It is the *quality* of things which is most affected by the Way. Often the quality of things is not readily seen, and therefore not appreciated. This is particularly true of the Way.

The Way of life offers no material benefits. No increase in wages. No new car. No marketable skill. Benefits *do* exist, but because they enhance the mind, body, and spirit, they are intangible. The unification of mind and body cannot be seen. A strong spirit is invisible. If no one can bear witness to these attributes, who will reward them? The answer is no one. Most will agree that a unified mind and body has its own rewards, as does a strong spirit. But those seeking the praise of their peers will not value these rewards. Perhaps this is why the Way is more often talked about than followed. Knowing that such talk is against the true nature of the Way, Lao-tzu wrote: ''False teachers of life use flowery words and start nonsense.''

It can be seen from the masters' discourse that true knowledge of the Way is accumulated over many years of study, or perhaps ''non-study.'' Yamamoto told of a young boy who wished to become the finest swordsman in the land. When the lad expressed his desire to learn quickly, he was cautioned by the master that a student in a hurry learns slowly. Andrew Lum mentioned that in meditation one must think without thinking. Lao-tzu has spoken of those who act without effort and of those who try without trying. All this points to a kind of non-doing which is associated with the Way. This has confused those who attempt to learn about the Way vicariously. The Way must be experienced.

Yamamoto gave us a clue to the Way when talking about ki. He said, ''...the principles of ki are quite well-known secrets. What not so well known is practice.'' Lao-tzu expressed the same thought in slightly different words. Knowing that what is obvious is often ignored or taken for granted, he wrote in the *Tao Te Ching:* ''My words are easy to understand and easy to perform, yet no man under heaven knows them or practices them.''

Yukiso Yamamoto, Lily Siou, and Andrew Lum actively incorporate the tenets of the Way into their daily life and thought. Anyone determined to seek the Way will have to do likewise.

What is firmly established
    cannot be uprooted.
What is firmly grasped
    cannot slip away.
It will be honored
    from generation to generation.
    Lao-tzu

Photo Subjects

Karen Harimoto: 23
Randall Tong: 24–25
John L. Miller: 28–29
Cherryll Kau, Nonna Loo, Clifford Wright: 46–47
Jason and Joyce Yamamoto: 50–51, 53
Wesley Martin: 83
Martha Carr: 84–85, 86–87
Charlotte Kim, Francis and Leslie Pang: 114–115
Dennis Iwanaga: 125, 126–127
Barbara S. Hartman: 136–137

Acknowledgments

The author has learned useful things about
photography from the Aesthetic Realism of Eli Siegel,
and he wishes to thank Ken Kimmelman, Dorothy Koppelman,
Dr. Arnold Perey, the Aesthetic Realism Photographers,
and Ed Green for their kind criticism.

Special thanks are also extended to June Boranian,
Sandy Brooke, George Chaplin, Bill Garrett, Flora
Inatsuka, Estrelita and Yousuf Karsh, Frank and
Lynne and Michael Lerner, Carl Linquist, Nonna Loo,
Eric Ono, Stan Sala, Mary and Tom Smith, Koichi
Tohei, and the Drama Department of the University
of Hawaii.

The assistance of Hawaiian Airlines, Robert's
Hawaiian Tours, the Hana Kai, Kula Lodge, and
Volcano House is also acknowledged.